▼
▼
▼
▼
▼
▼
▼
▼
▼
▼
▼
▼
▼
▼
▼
▼

"AFFAiR-PROOF"
YOUR MARRiAGE

"AFFAIR-PROOF" YOUR MARRIAGE

UNDERSTANDING, PREVENTING AND SURVIVING AN AFFAIR

▼

LANA STAHELI, PH.D.

Cliff Street Books

An Imprint of HarperPerennial
A Division of HarperCollins*Publishers*

A hardcover edition of this book was published in 1997 by HarperCollins Publishers under the title *Triangles*.

This book was originally published in 1995 by Staheli, Inc.

HarperCollins books may be purchased for educational, business, or sales promotional use. For information please write: Special Markets Department, HarperCollins Publishers, Inc., 10 East 53rd Street, New York, NY 10022.

First Cliff Street Book / Harper Perennial edition published 1998.

Designed by Nancy Singer

The Library of Congress has catalogued the hardcover edition as follows:

Staheli, Lana.
    Triangles : understanding, preventing and surviving
an affair / Lana Staheli. — 1st ed.
        p.   cm.
    ISBN 0-06-018758-1
    1. Adultery. 2. Married people—Sexual behavior. I. Title.
HQ806.S76   1997
306.73'6—dc20   96-34101

ISBN 0-06-092918-9 (pbk.)

99 00 01 02 ❖/RRD 10 9 8 7 6 5 4 3 2

To Lynn Taylor Staheli;

He is the love of my life

"A marriage is not a
love affair—and
a love affair is not
a marriage!"

—Joseph Campbell

Contents

Acknowledgments *xi*

Introduction *xiii*

PART 1   FACTS ON AFFAIRS

1   Human Nature and Affairs:
A Brief History 3

2   Facts Everyone Should Know
About Affairs 9

3   Men's Affairs 21

4   Women's Affairs 29

PART 2   THE NEEDS AND DRIVES
THAT PROMPT AFFAIRS

5   The Physiology and Psychology
of Affairs 49

6   Types of Affairs and the
    Needs They Meet   61

PART 3   INFORMATION AND ADVICE FOR
         THE AFFAIREE   79

7   Costs and Consequences   81

8   An Affair Is Just an Affair   85

9   Ending the Affair   101

10 Changing Course: Leaving Your
    Marriage to Be with Your Lover   105

11 Facts on Divorce   113

12 Refocusing on Your Marriage   125

PART 4   ADVICE FOR SPOUSES ON COPING
         WITH AN AFFAIR   135

13 Perspective   137

14 Discovery: Options for Dealing
    with a Spouse's Affair   145

15 Coping with the Shock and Trauma   165

PART 5   ADVICE FOR THE COUPLE:
         AFFAIR-PROOF YOUR MARRIAGE   187

16 What Is an Affair-Proof Marriage?   189

17 Strengthening Communication   205

18 Affair Proof Your Marriage:
    Be Each Other's Lover   219

    Conclusion   235

    Bibliography   *241*

Acknowledgments

I want to thank Lynn Taylor Staheli, M.D., who coaxed me to do this project and taught me how to organize my material and thoughts. He shared his computer knowledge and equipment. He is an inspiring teacher who is intelligent, creative, principled and altruistic. Lynn is my best friend, my lover and husband. He is a truly generous and extraordinary man.

Three friends were essential in producing "*Affair-Proof*" *Your Marriage*. They gave of their extraordinary talents and expertise without hesitation, time after time. They are Greg Hawes, Judy Dreis and Jeanne Brunette.

I appreciate the love, support, and advice of my family: Mildred Ribble, Letha Staheli, Todd Staheli, Diane Staheli, Linda Staheli, David Abramowitz and Bruce and Kim Ribble.

I am grateful to those who generously donated their time and energy to help me create this book: Mary Jane

Hansen, Charlene Butler, Deb Healy, Suzanne Peterson, A. Jean Crawford, David McFadden, Sharon Lee, Linda Kowalski, Lee Ellis and Alan Edelson. I appreciate our son, Todd, for making sure all the graphs accurately reflect the data.

Everything in our life works better because of our life-support system: Juli Verdieck, Sue Chadderton, Emily Wilson and Jay Wente. Marc Weinstein's work in research support was very valuable.

I thank my freelance team: Angela Turk, Brandy Poirer, Charles Reidy, June Rugh and Gary Graf for their technical and creative efforts on the first edition of *"Affair-Proof" Your Marriage*.

I want the information in *"Affair-Proof" Your Marriage* to be accessible to people and toward that goal I am indebted to Carey Quan Gelernter, *Seattle Times* staff reporter, who wrote a very informative article, *When the Heart Strays,* which was syndicated by Knight-Ridder and appeared in newspapers throughout the country.

I appreciate the work of my editors, Diane Reverand and Meaghan Dowling, and the others at HarperCollins who worked on *"Affair-Proof" Your Marriage*. It has been a pleasure to work with these extraordinarily talented people. I am delighted with the work of my agent, Patti Breitman, who is warm, efficient and effective.

Introduction

I hope the information in *"Affair-Proof" Your Marriage* will give you perspective on love, sex and infidelity. I explain why affairs happen and offer advice on how to avoid or resolve this painful situation. My book offers advice to affairees on what and what not to expect from an affair. I also suggest how to "affair-proof" your marriage!

Nearly everyone knows someone who has had an extramarital affair. Affairs touch over 60% of all marriages. Most people do not believe they or their spouse would have an affair, but the facts say otherwise. Anyone can be a casualty of an affair. No one is immune.

Sixty percent of marriages are affected by extramarital affairs. We all need to know the facts.

Men and women, singles and couples alike, should know the facts:

- ▶ Those who have affairs are more likely to divorce.
- ▶ 80% of those who divorce during an affair ultimately regret their decision.
- ▶ Affairees rarely marry one another, and those who do— divorce again.

Single men and women should know that waiting for a married lover to divorce leads to disappointment and heartbreak. Those who are happily married should know that marital happiness does not eliminate the possibility of an affair. Those who are even mildly unhappy should take heed—affairs are commonplace, easy and devastating. If you are unhappy with your marriage, it is far better to work to resolve the marriage problems or end the marriage before starting a new relationship. Affairs do not solve problems.

I wrote *"Affair-Proof" Your Marriage* because marriages all around me were being rocked by affairs. In the course of one year three of our friends divorced and in each situation one of the spouses was having an affair. In my counseling practice ten couples were struggling with affair-related problems. Affairs do break up marriages. For instance, our friends Ed and Lisa seemed to have a strong, loving marriage. Then Ed met Sarah during a business trip. They chatted over a drink and agreed to have dinner the following night. After dinner Sarah invited Ed to her room. They had the most incredible sex Ed had ever experienced. Six weeks later Ed asked Lisa, his wife of fourteen years, for a divorce. Ed was consumed with thoughts of Sarah and could not imagine his life without her.

Lisa had always feared divorce. Her life was so much better than she ever expected that she thought it could never last. Her fears led her to be quick and aggressive in pursuit of the divorce she didn't want. She explained, "I can't just stand by and let this happen to me. I have to do something. Every day is agony, and the nights seem to last forever."

We watched as our friends' lives were shattered. Lisa was gripped by depression and anxiety. Sarah was worried that Ed's friends would turn him against her so she insisted he choose between them and her, creating loneliness and alienation for Ed.

Four years after their divorce Lisa has rebuilt her life. She says, "I miss Ed desperately. It is still hard for me to believe this has happened to us. I don't even know what to regret, because I don't know what went wrong. I thought we were happy. We had our spats but we were good friends."

Lisa has dated a few men over the past years but finds it difficult to have confidence in a man or in a relationship.

Ed has gained a lot of weight and spends most of his time working. As for Sarah, her friends say she worries that someday Ed will leave *her*. Sarah entertains several times a week trying to make new friends and keep Ed busy.

As much as I wanted to help my friends, I could not refer them to any "facts" on what usually happens, on what to do, how to cope or how to fight for their marriage. I don't know if divorce was the right choice for Ed but I am sure the way he went about it was more destructive than necessary.

I wrote *"Affair-Proof" Your Marriage* to provide a condensed review of the research facts with the hope that it will save you from the agony Ed and Lisa experienced. Some facts are clearer than others. It is clear that most affairs last between two and three years. On the other hand, no one knows exact numbers when it comes to people's sexual behavior. A sampling of studies shows that the number of people who have had extramarital affairs ranges from 25% to 72%. Studies reflecting the general population show a lower frequency of affairs than those drawing from a more affluent population. For example, when upper income subscribers to *Playboy* or *New Woman* are queried, a higher incidence of infidelity is reported. In her 1989 book *Women and Love*, Shere Hite, Ph.D., reported that 70% of women married more than five years had admitted to extramarital sex. The respondents to this survey were more affluent and better educated than the American population as a whole.

The Kinsey Report found that the first time people were asked if they had been unfaithful 30% admitted they had. When they were questioned more thoroughly, another 30%

CHART 1   **Results from Surveys on Percentage of People Who Have Extramarital Sex**

Survey	Men	Women
1948 Kinsey Report 5,000 men 6,000 women	50%	26%
1970's Hunt Survey 691 men 740 women	41%	25%
1983 American Couples 3,638 men 3,634 women	29%	25%
Hite Report 1981 7,000 men 1987 4,500 women	72%	70%
1993 Janus Report 1,347 men 1,418 women	33%	25%

confessed to extramarital sex, bringing the total to 60%, indicating a reluctance to admit to infidelity even for a scientific survey. While I don't know the exact percentage of marriages affected by infidelity, I think the percentage of people under 60 who have affairs is 50–60% for men and 40–50% for women.

"Affair-Proof" Your Marriage is focused on a middle- and upper-income group ($50,000/year+) because my clients are mostly from this group. I have presented information from current research in sociological and psychological literature, including scientific studies as well as magazine surveys. Magazine surveys are an important source as they represent large numbers of people and include descriptions of their experiences.

"Affair-Proof" Your Marriage begins with "the facts" and a brief history of affairs to give perspective. Next, I divide affairs into types to allow you to make important distinctions between love affairs and sex affairs. Based on my counseling experience, I make suggestions for how to cope with an affair as an affairee or a spouse. I conclude *"Affair-Proof" Your Marriage* with suggestions on how you can protect your marriage from infidelity.

▼ DEFINITIONS

Affair   A sexually or emotionally intimate relationship between two people not married to one another.

Affairee   Either of the individuals involved in an affair. I coined this term because it has neither a positive nor negative connotation.

Adultery   Voluntary sexual intercourse between a married person and someone other than their spouse.

Fidelity   Adherence to the marriage contract of sexual exclusivity.

Monogamy   Having one spouse at a time.

Polygyny   Having more than one wife at a time.

Spouse   The individual married to the affairee, not the partner involved in the affair.

▼ How to Use This Guide

"Affair-Proof" Your Marriage provides information in a condensed form and is oriented toward offering perspective and advice on coping with and preventing affairs.

Part One gives a perspective on affairs. It includes a history, a description of the current status of affairs, their frequency, who has them and why.

Part Two explains the physiological and psychological needs that drive affairs.

Part Three is for affairees. It describes the types of affairs and the needs they meet, their joys, sorrows and consequences.

Part Four is for the spouse whose mate is involved in an affair, and provides ways to cope with the shock and trauma of the discovery, as well as advice on how to confront or sabotage the affair.

Finally, Part Five offers the couple information and advice on insulating their marriage and building trust by developing new skills, learning to understand one another's needs and feelings and creating growth within the marriage. This section suggests ways to affair-proof your marriage by being each other's lover.

"Affair-Proof" Your Marriage offers insights and advice from my experience during the last twenty years in counseling over 1,000 individuals and 500 couples. For clarity, I have given examples of individuals who have faced issues related to affairs. All names and specific details of actual circumstances have been changed to maintain confidentiality. Any similarities are purely coincidental.

Use *"Affair-Proof" Your Marriage* to Learn About Affairs; Ignorance Is Not Bliss

1. I suggest you read through the book. Then go back and highlight the parts you want to remember.
2. Charts and graphs are used extensively to provide information quickly and visually.
3. *"Affair-Proof" Your Marriage* is an abbreviated reference. After reading the book and looking at the graphs, go back to the recommended reading section and read the books listed to gain more in-depth information on a particular subject.
4. Use *"Affair-Proof" Your Marriage* to gain perspective on your affair.
5. Learn the skills recommended for creating intimacy in your marriage by practicing them—daily.
6. Refer to *"Affair-Proof" Your Marriage* to create a lasting, loving marriage that is secure.

I hope you will find *"Affair-Proof" Your Marriage* a useful resource guide that can be quickly and easily read. Please use the bibliography and recommended reading list to delve deeper into the areas that interest you.

PART 1

Facts on Affairs

▶ 1

Human Nature and Affairs: A Brief History

History provides perspective. While we readily assume that marriages have always been based on fidelity, historically fidelity is not the norm. In fact, the idea of being sexually faithful to one spouse throughout life is relatively new and accepted by only part of current world cultures. For example, Persian, African, Chinese, Japanese, Roman and Greek cultures all allowed men more than one wife or legitimized extramarital sexual relationships for some period in their history.

Rules or laws governing sexual behavior were based either on legal rights or religious doctrine. Legal marriage was reserved for the upper class whose property and lineage were valued by society. In Egypt common people were first allowed to marry in about 2,000 B.C., and adultery applied primarily to women.

Jewish sexual mores were originally developed to encourage men to take responsibility for the survival of women and children. In the early Jewish culture, beginning around 500 B.C., marriage was not a legal entity but the couple was recognized as married within their community. The purpose of this marriage was reproduction. If a child was not produced, the

CHART 2   **Percentage of Cultures that Mandate Monogyny**
Murdock 1967; van den Berghe 1979; Betzig 1986

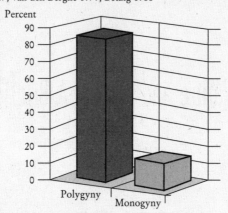

Eighty-four percent of societies permit men to have more than one wife at a time. However, only about 5% of men in these cultures practice polygyny.

marriage was dissolved. If an older brother died without producing sons, his younger brother was required to marry the widow. Roman marriage ceremonies were acts of initiation with sexual activity beginning when a girl was twelve and a boy fourteen. Romans viewed sex as a natural force that should be unrestrained. In most ancient cultures, fidelity was not expected of men or women.

Strict Christian sexual codes were not defined until four centuries after the death of Christ. Saint Augustine had a major influence on the sexual attitudes of his followers. He began to advocate chastity in about A.D. 400, after his conversion to Christianity. Prior to his conversion, he had loved his mistress with whom he had a son. His mother forbade their marriage. His writings show that before his Christian conversion, he had prayed to God, saying, "Give me chastity and continency but do not give it yet."

CHART 3   **Percentage of Cultures That Accept Some
Type of Affairs**

Ford & Beach, 1951

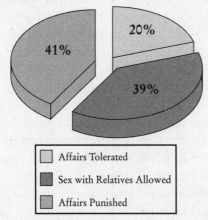

The majority of human societies allow extramarital sexual relations with restrictions.

Saint Augustine claimed that celibacy was the greatest good, and intercourse between husband and wife should be exclusively for procreation. Saint Augustine's beliefs mark the origin of sex being considered a sin within Christian doctrine. Christian leaders began to dictate very limited parameters for sexual behavior. The concepts of adultery and the desirability of celibacy did not become part of the Christian code until the eleventh century. It was during this time that marriage became sacred and divorce forbidden.

A few feudal European societies allowed the lord *jus primary noctis,* or "the right of the first night," portrayed in the movie *Braveheart.* This ruling gave a lord the right to have sex with the bride of his subject on their wedding night, if he so desired.

During the sixth century A.D., the Arab prophet Mohammed celebrated and encouraged sex with spouses.

Mohammed raised the status of women by requiring marriage between couples rather than allowing men to own their women. He rejected the idea of affairs and wanted his followers to channel their sexual drives within marriage. Men were encouraged to have as many as four wives at a time. The husband was to circulate among them on consecutive nights and he was to provide for them equally. Divorce, *Talaqus-Sunna*, was easy, originating in pre-Islamic times. Announcing "I divorce thee; I divorce thee; I divorce thee," then abstaining from sex for three months ended the marriage.

Traditional Chinese and Japanese men had multiple wives or concubines, while women were expected to remain faithful to their husbands to protect the family lineage.

Eskimo peoples considered sex to be an extension of friendship. Sexual relations with a wife were a gift from one man to another but only if the wife was willing. Reciprocity was expected.

Helen Fisher, Ph.D., surveyed sixty-two cultures to identify their beliefs about love. She provides both a historical and current perspective in her book *Anatomy of Love*. Dr. Fisher cites examples of infidelity in cultures along the Xingu River in Brazil, where it is openly discussed and celebrated, and in communities along the Adriatic Coast in Italy, where nearly every man has a lover but secrecy is the rule.

Several religious groups in America experimented with dictating the sexual behavior of their members. One of the most sexually restrictive groups was the Shakers, who demanded celibacy of their members. The Oneida Colony, on the other hand, was one of the most permissive, and advocated "free love," or sex for pleasure, by appointment with mutual consent. During the nineteenth century, many Mormon men were allowed more than one wife and were expected to be sexually faithful to their wives.

No religious system in the world has succeeded in harnessing human sexual drives and eliminating infidelity.

"The man or woman who commits adultery should be given 100 strokes of the whip. The whipping must be witnessed by a group of believers or on television."
—LIBYAN LEADER MOAMMAR KADDHAFI,
CAIRO, EGYPT, APRIL 3, 1995

The Puritans of the sixteenth and seventeenth centuries are often wrongly accused of sexual oppression. In fact, their sexual restrictions were very relaxed, and their members were not driven out of society because of their sexual behavior. Nathaniel Hawthorne's classic novel *The Scarlet Letter* is simply a work of fiction.

Recent studies show that women in all cultures chose to have multiple sexual partners when given the opportunity, suggesting that the lineage concerns of men were well-founded.

Every culture and each religion has its own history, values and traditions, and throughout history and without geographical boundaries, married people have had extramarital affairs.

► 2

Facts Everyone Should Know About Affairs

- ► Extramarital sex is a consistent feature in the history of humankind.

- ► Nearly 60% of middle and upper income married couples will be affected by an extramarital affair.

- ► Women are becoming as likely as men to have an affair.

- ► Religion is not a deterrent to affairs.

- ► The "in love" sensation is caused by the increased production of an amphetamine-like chemical known as PEA. It creates an intense but temporary feeling.

- ► Psychological needs play a role in affairs.

- ► Love affairs are different from sex affairs.

- ► Men and women have love affairs for the same reasons but sex affairs for different reasons.

- ► Around 15% of women and 25% of men have more than four affairs during their married life.

- ► Most love affairs last between two and three years but some last a lifetime.

▸ Fewer than 10% of affairees divorce their spouse, then marry their lover.

▸ Nearly 80% of those who divorce because of an affair are sorry later.

▸ Over 75% of affair-marriages end in divorce.

▸ For those whose marriages survive affairs, recovery takes between one and three years.

▸ Getting rid of the spouse does not get rid of the pain.

▸ Healing from a divorce takes about three years, children pay a high price, and many spouses remain bitter for decades.

▸ Most marriages survive an affair. If you want to stay married, you can.

Americans in the 1990s have affairs as commonly as our neighbors around the world. Considering our long history of infidelity and the high percentage of marriages affected by affairs, it is important to be realistic and informed. No marriage is safely insulated from an affair.

The sociological definition of marriage is a relationship within which a group socially approves of and encourages sexual intercourse and the birth of children. It may or may not have religious significance. Marriage is recognized in every known culture, although the rules and expectations vary. For some it is a child-rearing institution, for others it is companionship and for many it is true and everlasting love. This same desire for an intensely passionate lifetime love often leads to affairs.

"The institution of marriage is in peril. There is no society in the world where people have stayed married without enormous community pressure to do so."
—MARGARET MEAD

The majority of studies cited in *"Affair-Proof" Your Marriage* are focused on the middle and upper socioeconomic group. The evidence indicates a difference in people's sexual behaviors and attitudes related to their education and affluence. For example, the 1994 study by Edward Laumann, Ph.D., known as the Sex in America Survey, reported that 23% of their population had a college education and only 27% of men and 8% of women had more than eleven sexual partners. *The Janus Report*, in which 37% of respondents were college educated, indicated that 61% of the men and 55% of women had more than eleven sex partners throughout their lifetime.

Men and women with more resources have greater control over their time, energy and money. They also have more sexual freedom.

CHART 4   Number of Lifetime Sexual Partners Reported by Studies Representing Different Socioeconomic Groups

Janus, 1993; Laumann, 1994

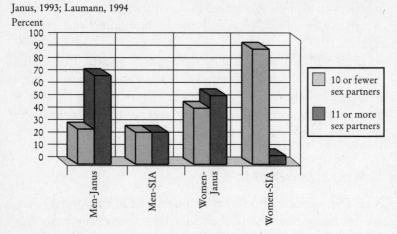

Janus Report, College = 37%; Sex in America, College = 23%

CHART 5   **Belief in the Importance of Fidelity Among Married Couples**

Blumstein & Schwartz, 1983

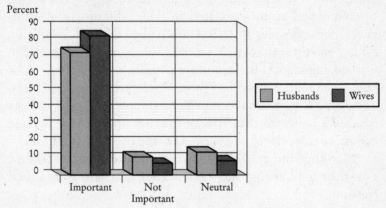

Husbands and wives believe they should be faithful to their spouse.

▼ MOST PEOPLE BELIEVE IN SEXUAL FIDELITY, BUT . . .

Marriages are usually based on a commitment to sexual fidelity, which is an explicit agreement that neither partner will become intimately involved, physically or emotionally, with anyone else.

Philip Blumstein, Ph.D., and Pepper Schwartz, Ph.D., in a survey of 20,000 people, found that the vast majority of married people believe that sexual exclusivity with one another is an important cornerstone of marriage and *most people are faithful to their spouses most of the time.*

▼ WHO HAS AFFAIRS?

Men and women who feel their physical and emotional needs are not being met well in their marriage have affairs more frequently than those who believe their needs are being satisfied in their marriage. People who live in large cities on the East or West coasts of the United States have a higher incidence of affairs than those who live in rural middle America.

Opportunity, education and control over time make a person more prone to having extramarital affairs. People who are accountable for their time to either their spouse, employers or families are the least likely to have extramarital affairs.

▼ AFFAIRS START EARLIER IN MARRIAGE

A 1983 study, *American Couples,* by Blumstein and Schwartz, showed that 29% of married people under 25 years old had had an affair, with no statistical difference between the number of men and women who chose to be unfaithful to their spouses early in life. In the 1950s, 9% of spouses under 25 had been involved in extramarital sex.

CHART 6

Researchers	Who Has Affairs
Richardson, 1985	Married men with single women
Quinn, 1987	Employed people
Macklin, 1980	Middle class educated women
Spanier & Margolis, 1983	Those who had premarital sex
Spanier & Margolis, 1983	Those with lower quality sex life
Spanier & Margolis, 1983	Those with lower quality marriage
Stehan & McMullin, 1982	Those who live in large cities

CHART 7   **Infidelity Among Married Couples
Who Are Less Than 25 Years Old**
Blumstein & Schwartz, 1983

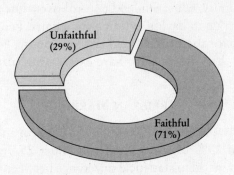

*Extramarital affairs start before spouses are 25 years of age, without
much difference between men and women.*

A *Playboy* magazine survey found young wives in their 20s
to be more sexually active outside their marriage than their
husbands. Independence and birth control had given them
opportunities formerly available only to men. When given the
chance, women have affairs as readily as men.

▼ FEW BELIEVE IN OPEN MARRIAGE

In the 1970s, Nena and George O'Neill promoted the idea of
open marriage, meaning that a couple would agree that each
was free sexually or emotionally for intimate relationships
with others without lies or deceit.

In the case of Marla and Jerry, Marla says, "Jerry was
always more sexual than I. I don't mind sex but I don't crave
it like he does. What is important to me is that we are good

parents and that we enjoy the lifestyle we have together. We have an open marriage. I know he has sex with other girls. I don't always know who but I usually know when. We have a code, when he says he is 'playing ball,' I know he is with someone. He always uses a condom and he is committed to our family. Several of our friends have affairs and lie about it. I couldn't stand that."

Marla admits that she believes Jerry is going to have extramarital sex with or without her agreement and she feels more confident and secure in their marriage knowing when he is having an affair. Many couples find deceit more difficult to cope with than infidelity.

The option of choosing open marriage as a way of preventing divorce has not been successful. More than half of these open marriages ended in divorce, including the

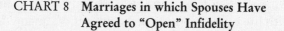

CHART 8   **Marriages in which Spouses Have Agreed to "Open" Infidelity**

Lawson, 1988

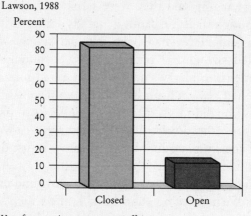

Very few marriages are open to affairs.

O'Neills'. Open marriage is not widespread. Studies indicate that fewer than 15% of couples are currently in marriages where they agree that it is acceptable to pursue sex outside their marriage. *Most partners deceive their spouse rather than negotiate an open marriage.*

▼ Swinging

Swinging is the term used to describe comarital sex involving both the husband and wife together with others. About 5% of married couples have been involved in swinging at some time.

Swinging may include group sex but is generally a three-some. Men seldom have intercourse with one another. Richard Jenks, Ph.D., found, contrary to popular assumption, that swingers were not distinctly more liberal or deviant than non-swingers. Swingers were often more conservative on political issues than nonswingers. The swingers surveyed were as satisfied with their jobs, friends, health, income and education as nonswingers. Swingers were more happy with their sex life and with life in general than nonswingers. Women who participated in swinging said they were satisfied with this arrangement, although their husbands generally initiated it.

Krista and Harry had been married sixteen years when they started swinging. Krista explains, "I found some sexual advertisements in Harry's den. When I asked him about them he said it had always been his fantasy to have sex with other women but he didn't want to hurt me. We both liked sex and we both had other lovers during our marriage. We hated the lying and sneaking around. I agreed to try it just once, saying if I didn't like it we would quit.

"We signed up with a swinging club we found in a swingers magazine. We met at a neighborhood home which had two hot tubs. I was pretty nervous but it was fun. It wasn't lewd or pressured.

CHART 9   Profiles of Couples Who Participate Together in
           Sexual Relationships with Others

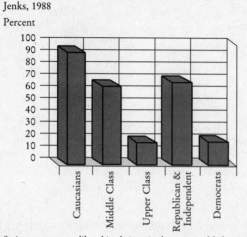

Jenks, 1988

Percent

*Swingers are more liberal in their attitudes on sexual behavior
and more conservative on political issues.*

"If either of us (or both of us) finds a partner we like, we
have sex. Sometimes together, other times separately. There are
times we choose each other. We have met new friends and we
have a good time. I'm glad we share this time together. I actually feel more secure being with him and knowing what is
going on. I know he won't fall in love and want a divorce—
which has happened to some of our friends. This is just sex."

Krista and Harry's attitudes about swinging are typical of
swingers. They believe sex with other partners is desirable and
they don't want to lie or cheat. They see their form of sexual
expression as something they share with one another, not
something that comes between them.

▼ WHERE?

The woman's home is the first choice as a place for lovers to
rendezvous. The second most frequent location for an affair is

CHART 10 **Places for Extramarital Sex**

Lawson, 1988

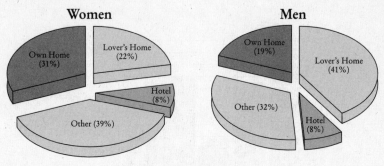

the man's home. Hotels were used as a primary meeting place by only 8% of those surveyed. Other places for an affair include the home of a friend, a boat, camper, car, office or the park.

▼ AFFAIRS LAST A COUPLE OF YEARS

Studies in the early 1950s showed that 65% of women's affairs lasted less than four years. A 1987 study by Trish Hall, published in the *New York Times,* surveyed 200 men and women and found that their affairs lasted an average of two years.

Affairs go through transitions over time. They may begin as romantic, sexual or emotional relationships and may become intimate friendships. Affairs that become friendships can last decades or a lifetime. Regardless of the strength of desire, most affairs dissolve over time when the feelings soften and the complexity of the affair is emotionally and physically draining.

CHART 11
Hall, 1987

	Duration of Affair
Women	21 months
Men	29 months

▼ MULTIPLE AFFAIRS

People who have affairs are likely to have more than one, especially men. Two-thirds of the men surveyed who had affairs had more than one. Women averaged between one and three affairs. About 25% of men and 15% of women who have affairs have four or more.

CHART 12 **Average Number of Affairs for Men and Women Who Have Affairs**

Blumstein & Schwartz, 1983

Percent

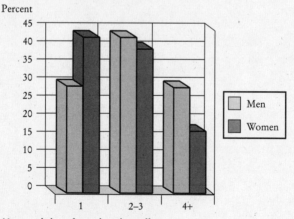

Most people have fewer than three affairs.

▶ 3

Men's Affairs

"Men like women with a past because they hope history will repeat itself."

—MAE WEST

Several studies show that between 70% and 80% of affluent men have extramarital sex sometime during their married life.

Men have always been involved in extramarital affairs and have often considered themselves *entitled* to multiple lovers. The purpose of marriage was to provide heirs, not love, romance or sex. The drive to mate with multiple partners is alluring to many men, and those men who can provide the most resources to a woman and her offspring have more choices of when, how often and with whom they have sex.

American men are reportedly more sexually faithful than European or Asian men, but recent surveys cast doubt on this assumption. Over the past four decades the number of American men acknowledging their participation in affairs has risen from 50% to as high as 84%. These extramarital dalliances include sex with prostitutes as well as lifetime lovers.

CHART 13   **Percentage of Middle and Upper Income Men Who
Had an Affair over the Past Three Decades**

Kinsey, 1953; Hunt, 1970; Hite, 1981; *Marriage and Divorce*, 1987; Halper, 1988.

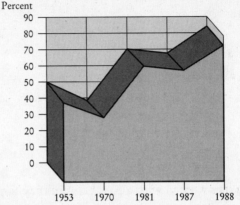

Multiple studies in the 1980s report over 70% of affluent men have had an affair, compared to between 40% and 50% prior to the mid 1970s.

▼ MORE MEN HAVE AFFAIRS

The Hite Report on Male Sexuality, which surveyed over 7,000 men, says that men start extramarital sex early in their marriage, and over 70% have an affair sometime during their married life.

Opportunity and birth control are two major factors cited as causes of this increase. Men who work 8 A.M. to 5 P.M. and go directly home after work may simply not have the discretionary time for an affair. Birth control has given some men the belief that they can have sex without the worry of an unwanted pregnancy.

Wives often erroneously believe that their husbands could not be having an affair because "he just doesn't have time." Many men have an explanation for their time away from home that allows them ample time for affairs.

In Larry's case, he says, "I travel quite a bit so sex is easy. I just tell my wife I'm on an earlier flight than I am, so I can go spend a few hours or the night with my lover."

Gene explains it this way, "I just like being with two lovers. My wife is great in and out of bed but I like variety. I'm a little overweight and we are very religious so my wife would never expect me to have a lover. When I go bird hunting with my friend Chuck, we board the dogs in a kennel and take our girlfriends on vacation instead. Often to a little island in the Caribbean, occasionally to Hong Kong or Europe. The girls love it and my wife never knows. Besides, she doesn't like to fly."

Lou has what he considers an ideal situation for himself. "I don't have to lie to my wife. I date during the lunch hour or early afternoon. Nobody really knows exactly where I am, so

CHART 14 **Percentage of Men Who Are Unfaithful by Years of Marriage**

Hite, 1981

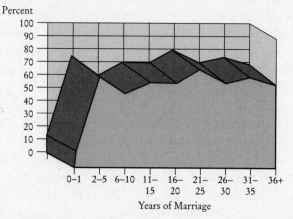

Seventy-two percent of men married more than two years say they had extramarital sex.

I just say 'I'm out to a meeting' or 'I'm making sales calls.' Sometimes a lover comes to my office. I like the danger of getting away with the forbidden."

Realistically, affairs don't require large blocks of time. Men who want to have affairs will find the time. These men believe that their desire for multiple sex partners is natural and normal for them but not for their wives.

▼ MEN'S REASONS FOR AFFAIRS

Traditionally, men think of sex as being separate from love. They are more likely than women to think of sex as recreation, a conquest or fun.

Their affairs are often sporadic and opportunistic. The affair may be as simple as a single sexual encounter while traveling or an occasional tryst while their wife is out of town.

Wives may be surprised to find out that their husbands may have sex affairs because of the husband's sexual problems. While men may have difficulty achieving an erection or ejaculate prematurely with their wife, they may have no difficulty when they are with someone with whom they have no emotional involvement.

Hank says, "I'm a physical kind of guy and I like women. I grew up thinking sex was only for marriage and was hard to get. Wow, was I surprised at how many women are ready, willing and able. I always make it clear I love my wife, I'm married, and I'm planning to stay that way. I don't usually have to lie, I just tell my wife I have a meeting and will be a little late."

Hank clearly separates his desire for sex from his feelings of love for his wife. He sees no conflict between his commitment to his wife and his affairs. Like most men, Hank's reason for an affair is simple—more sex. The reasons I hear men give for their affairs are primarily sexual.

▼

Top 7 Reasons Men Have Affairs

1. Sexual variety—he enjoys more than one sex partner
2. More sex—greater quantity of sex
3. Opportunity—a woman is available for sex and he believes he won't get caught
4. Challenge—he enjoys the chase and the catch
5. Seduction—he enjoys flirting and romance
6. Wife unavailable—his wife is out of town, working late or has a recent pregnanacy
7. Sexual dysfunction—he has difficulty performing sexually with his wife but not with other partners

▼ ## "SUCCESSFUL" MEN HAVE AFFAIRS

"Successful" men, as defined by Jan Halper, Ph.D., have affairs more readily than the average income man. Dr. Halper interviewed 4,126 male business leaders, executives and professionals and reported the highest rate of affairs garnered from any survey: 88% of the men questioned acknowledged their involvement in at least one affair.

A 1995 Canadian study by Daniel Pérusse showed that single men with high income, education and job status had much busier sex lives than men with lower status. The high status men had sex with more different women more often than any other group of men.

The highest incidence of affairs is found among the following occupational groups: businessmen, professionals such as attorneys, physicians and dentists, executives, salesmen, pilots, truck drivers and sailors.

Multiple studies report that men with high incomes are

CHART 15   Percentage of "Successful" Men Who Are
Unfaithful During Their Married Life

Halper, 1988

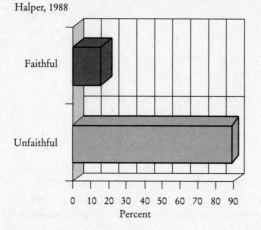

"Successful" men have the highest incidence of extramarital affairs.

more likely than men with lower incomes to have affairs.
Research and anecdotal evidence show that affluent men have
the greatest number of sexual partners before and during their
mariages.

▼ MEN HIRE PROSTITUTES

The Kinsey Institute New Report on Sex, published in 1991,
says that one-third of the men they surveyed acknowledged
having sex with a prostitute at least once in their lives. Oral sex
was the first choice and intercourse the second. While most
encounters with prostitutes are strictly sexual, some prostitutes report that their clients want conversation and affection.

The early Kinsey study of 1953 reported that two-thirds of
men said they had been to a prostitute, which may be related
to the number of men in military service during World War II

who were stationed away from home. Studies show that prostitution occurs in virtually every culture. In the United States the number of prostitutes is estimated to be about 250,000. Tokyo has upwards of 130,000, Poland 230,000, and in Germany (where prostitution is legal) over 50,000 prostitutes are registered.

Women often wonder, why do men have sex with prostitutes? Guy explains, "Because it is cheap. Surprised? I pay $70 to $100 bucks for a blow job. It feels good and no hassle. There's no talking, no dates, no future. Just good sex. I don't like to screw, because you don't know what you might take home—or if some year some kid might coming knocking on your door. I pay the money and when I'm done she leaves. I have a couple favorites but they are all pretty good."

The number of men having sex with prostitutes is further evidence of the importance of casual sex to men. Men find sex with a prostitute to be something very different from sex with someone they care about. Some men feel more free and more relaxed when there is no emotional relationship with their sexual partner.

CHART 16   **Percentage of Men Who Paid for Sex with a Prostitute at Least Once in Their Lives**

Reinisch, 1991

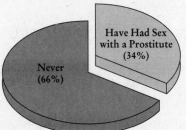

One-third of the men surveyed in the Kinsey Institute Study admitted to paying for sex with a prostitute at least once.

▶ 4

Women's Affairs

Women are every bit as willing as men to have an affair!

Women are partners in affairs. For those who believe women are intrinsically more faithful than men, current research shows that women engage in intercourse with multiple partners as readily as men when they have the freedom and opportunity.

A woman's sexuality has often been more feared than celebrated. Men throughout the world want to be certain they are the fathers of their heirs, and, as a result, women have been subjected to clitorectomy, whipping, beating, foot binding and even death to ensure sexual fidelity. In many cultures only women, not men, can be adulterers. Despite all the constraints and punishments, women have affairs.

Jane is a good example of a woman who never expected to have an affair but ultimately did take a lover. Jane was 34 and had been married for ten years when she started seeing Jeff. Her kids were all busy with school and activities, and her husband, Sam, always seemed tired. She felt overwhelmed by her new job and at the same time she felt lonely and bored.

She says, "I had met Jeff several times at various parties but this particular evening we talked for probably an hour. He had changed jobs about a year ago and he understood how difficult it is to be the new kid on the block. He commented he would be glad to have lunch although it might cause talk to be seen with such a pretty woman. Wow, it had been a long time since anyone had said I was pretty.

"I needed someone to talk to, a friend who understood the complexity of my new job. At least that's what I told myself. After about three months of lunches I invited him to my home for lunch saying I had some terrific leftover chili.

"We became lovers that afternoon. I felt five years younger. Jeff made me feel feminine and alive. We made each other laugh. We gave each other advice. He gave me some ideas on how to get Sam to be more active and involved with our family. Our affair has been good for my self-esteem. I feel better about myself than any other time in my life.

"It was never a consideration that either of us would divorce, although we both had our fantasies. Our affair lasted slightly less than three years. We are still good friends and he will always have a special place in my heart."

Women are usually insightful about their affairs, knowing exactly why they want a lover. Contemporary women are as sexually active outside their marriages as their foremothers, probably more so.

"As long as prehistoric females were secretive about their extramarital affairs, they could garner extra resources, life insurance, better genes and more varied DNA for their biological futures. Hence, those who sneaked into the bushes with secret lovers lived on—unconsciously passing on through centuries whatever it is in the female spirit that motivates modern women to philander."

—Helen Fisher, Ph.D.

▼ INCREASE IN WOMEN'S AFFAIRS

Surveys indicate that the percentage of women who have extramarital sex has increased during the last three decades. In 1953 Alfred Kinsey, Ph.D., found that 29% of married women admitted to at least one affair. A *Psychology Today* survey, in 1970, reported that 36% of their female readers had extramarital sex. In 1981 and 1982, *Cosmopolitan* magazine surveyed its readers and announced that 50% confessed to marital infidelity. In her 1989 report, *Women in Love,* Shere Hite, Ph.D., found that 70% of her respondents had been involved in an affair.

Not only has the number of women who have affairs increased, the age at which they have their first affair has decreased. In the 1950s and 1960s, women had their first affair during their 30s and early 40s. During the 1970s and 1980s, the highest rate of infidelity was among women between ages 26 and 30. Now, in the 1990s, women start affairs in their early 20s.

CHART 17   **Increase in the Percentage of Middle and Upper Income Women Who Had Affairs over the Past Four Decades**

Kinsey, 1953; Athanasiou, 1970; Wolfe, 1981; Hite, 1989

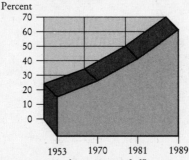

Several studies indicate an increase in the percentage of affluent women who admit to an affair over the past forty years.

▼ WHY DO WOMEN HAVE AFFAIRS?

Women have affairs for their own emotional gratification. They say their affairs enhance their self-esteem by giving them positive feedback, both physically and emotionally.

The women surveyed described their affairs as "fun," "casual," "a chance to know someone," or "just an affair." About 20% became involved in affairs just for sex. Dr. Ralph Meyering, Professor Emeritus at Illinois State University, notes, "Married women seem to see extramarital sex as something quite different from sex with their husbands. In sex outside of their marriages, women appear to feel freer to repudiate their repressions and explore their preferences."

Other reasons women have affairs include loneliness, the desire for adventure or experience, looking for a new husband or because their friends have affairs. Only 7% are retaliatory.

Becky, married to a physician for eighteen years, is having

CHART 18   **Reasons Women Give for Their Affairs**
Hite, 1989

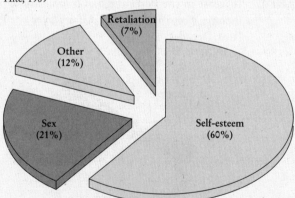

Women say the major reason for their affairs is to enhance their self-esteem.

an affair with a man nine years younger than herself. He works as a salesman in a car dealership. She says, "Gerard and I have fun. We like the same food, the same music, the same television programs and we laugh at the same things. He is a great guy and we have a ton of fun. I love Gerard as a friend but we certainly aren't in love with each other. I would miss him if we stopped seeing each other."

Becky cares about Gerard but does not feel in love with him. Their friendship and shared activities are the main focus of their affair. Women are more choosy about their husbands than about their lovers. While a woman will have an affair with a guy like Gerard, she wouldn't consider marrying him.

▼ ▬▬▬▬▬▬▬▬▬▬▬▬▬▬▬▬▬▬▬▬▬▬▬▬▬▬▬

Top 7 Reasons Women Have Affairs

1. Improves self-esteem—she enjoys the attention and compliments about her abilities as well as her body

2. New and varied sexual experience—she feels freer to experiment and explore with a lover than with her husband

3. Emotional connection—she desires emotional closeness and intimacy

4. Loneliness—she needs someone to talk with who will listen to her

5. Deeper understanding of self—she learns from exploring her feelings and thoughts with someone who cares for her

6. Feel younger and sexier—her lover's desire for her sexually makes her feel playful and free

7. Fear of aging—she is afraid getting older will eliminate her attractiveness to men

▬▬▬▬▬▬▬▬▬▬▬▬▬▬▬▬▬▬▬▬▬▬▬▬▬▬▬

▼ WOMEN ARE NOT SWEPT OFF THEIR FEET

Contrary to the romantic notion, women are not "swept off their feet" when they become involved in an affair. In fact, women are thoughtful. A 1982 study by Lynn Atwater, Ph.D., indicates that half the women she surveyed knew their affair partner for several months before beginning the affair; the other half knew them for a year or more. On average, they considered having an affair for at least a month before it began and usually discussed the possibility with a friend.

When asked who initiated their affair, one-fourth of the women said they initiated it and half said it was mutual. Men unilaterally initiated fewer than one-fourth of the affairs.

Paula married her first lover, Kenny. She said, "We married when we were 21 and I had didn't have sexual experience with anyone but Kenny. Kenny was a good lover but sex was pretty routine. You know, guy on top, girl on bottom. I bought a couple books, *Light Her Fire* and *Light His Fire.* I was stirred up just reading them. I couldn't get him to look at either one. When I tried a few things from the books he brushed me away, and laughed. He joked, 'You are becoming a kinky old lady.' I laughed but it hurt.

"I kept reading all the magazine stories about infidelity and I started thinking I would like to have a lover before I got too old. I always thought our attorney was especially friendly with me, so I made an appointment and told him my problem. He kissed me like I had never been kissed before right there in his office. He asked me if I wanted more. I did!

"Sex with him is erotic and dangerous. At a friend's dinner party he pulled me into the den and made love with me while the others sampled the hors d'oeuvres. Sometimes we meet at his office, the back of his car or on a blanket in the park. I hope this never ends. It's wild."

CHART 19   **Percentage of Affairs Initiated by Men, Women or by Mutual Effort**

Atwater, 1982

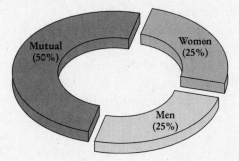

Women are as likely as men to initiate an affair but most attractions are mutual.

Paula is very clear about what her affair means to her. She is having fun and exploring herself sexually. She has no illusions of love or romance.

▼ WOMEN ARE NOT CONSUMED BY ROMANTIC LOVE

Women consider romance to be important in both marriage and affairs. However, over 80% say they care for their lover or consider him a friend but are not "in love" with him. Women seek emotional involvement in their affairs, but also limit the level of their feelings.

While sex occurs in most affairs, communication is a feature women value highly. Women want someone to talk to and confide in. Men are more verbally expressive with their lovers than with their wives.

May offers insight into why women choose to have affairs. May reflects, "I had just turned 40, had my tubes tied, lost twelve pounds and I felt free. I felt sexier than I did in my 20s and I wanted something new in my life. I wanted a lover.

"I knew a friend, Nancy, who had an affair three or four years ago and said it was great for her ego. We had lunch and I asked her if she was glad she had done it. She said it was wonderful, terrible, incredible and painful and she would do it again in a minute.

"I don't know if I decided then to invite Tad to my bed or if I had already made up my mind before my lunch with Nancy. I told her I was thinking about Tad, my son's coach. She agreed he would be a good choice because he was happily married, discreet and fun-loving. She thought he wouldn't turn me down. That gave me the courage to talk to Tad.

"I called Tad's office under the guise of raising money for the school and asked if we could meet. I got a sexy new dress and new lingerie and went to see Tad. I was nervous but I thought that if he turned me down he would be nice about it and he wouldn't tell anyone. Tad did not need much persuasion. We had great sex from the beginning. I love sex with Tad. When we go to a hotel we watch the adult movies while we make love. I had no idea sex could be so exciting. He has taught me to explore myself and him. We also like to talk to each other. We are close friends and confidantes. We talk about getting older, things we would like to do before we die, movies we like, our families—really everything."

May was restless although not unhappy in her marriage. She had friends who had affairs so she had given some thought to the idea. May took time to think about having an affair, which is more typical of women than men. By the time she initiated the affair, she knew whom she would choose and what she wanted from the affair.

May views her affair as being a good experience because her lover encourages her to explore and enjoy herself physically. While sex is a major focus of their affair, they also have a

CHART 20   **Married Women's Feelings for Their Lovers**
Atwater, 1982

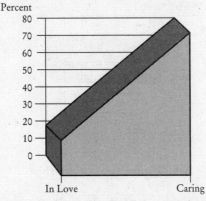

Married women report they care for their lover but are not in love with him.

caring and loving friendship. She believes her affair has a positive effect on her and her marriage.

▼ MARRIED WOMEN PREFER MARRIED MEN

Married women tend to have affairs with married men—rather than with single men—for several reasons. Married women and married men have a similar amount of discretionary time available. While much of their time may be committed to their families, both can secretly take a few hours to be together during the day, in the evening or on the weekend. Married women believe married men will not become overly dependent on them, that they won't tell and that they are less likely to have a sexually transmitted disease.

Wives believe this type of relationship adds to the stability of their marriage. They also believe their married lovers will be faithful to them.

CHART 21   **Percentage of Wives Affairs with Married or Single Men**

Cosmopolitan, August, 1981

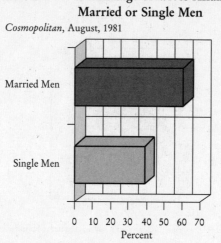

Married women choose married men as lovers.

▼ WORKING WOMEN

Women who are employed full-time outside the home are more likely to have an affair than full-time homemakers. Several studies have reported similar findings. Travis and Sadd reported that 47% of wives who were employed full-time and 27% of full-time homemakers had been involved in an affair before they were 40 years old.

New Woman magazine found that 57% of employed wives who had an affair met their lover at work.

Amy had an affair with her boss. She explains, "When I was promoted to head of accounting, Carl became my supervisor. He really took an interest in helping me. During the busy times he would come in and take part of my workload. It seemed like he was always there when I needed him. He started advising me on my career. He loaned me some of his own computer software so I would become more versatile and competitive. He started putting me on committees and helping me with special projects.

"We spent more and more time together. We talked about everything—families, friends, sports and my job. It just seemed natural we were lovers, too. When I got another promotion he was so proud of me and I knew he loved me. Even when the new job meant a move, he was there encouraging and supporting me. It has been about five years since I moved East but we talk by e-mail every week and I see him anytime I'm in the Bay Area. My only regret is I haven't found a younger single man like him."

Amy's affair with Carl is based on friendship and mutual respect. He is her mentor as well as her lover. When people are excited about their work, the energy between them can easily evolve into an affair.

CHART 22   **Percentage of Employed or Homemaker Wives Who Had an Affair**

Travis & Sadd, 1977

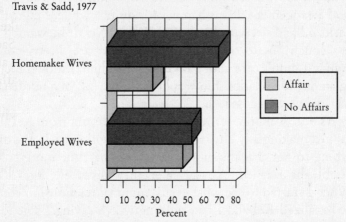

Wives who are employed full-time outside the home are more likely to have an affair than full-time homemakers.

▼ AFFAIRS TO SAVE MARRIAGES

In 1975, Linda Wolfe published *Playing Around* after she had studied twenty-one women who were having affairs to keep their marriages intact. The reasoning for many of these women was that if they could meet their own needs, their marriages would be more successful. Many said they were desperately lonely. Others were afraid, believing their husbands did not love them or were not committed to their marriage. Five years after the initial study, only three of the twenty-one women were still married.

In Jessica's words, "I felt so alone. I thought it was supposed to be the man who always wanted sex. Not in our marriage. I could not even get Kel to respond to sex, let alone talk to me. He complained I was always wanting something from him. He reminded me that I knew he was a loner before we got married. True, but I didn't really know what that would mean in terms of our relationship.

"Finally I decided to have an affair with our neighbor. He was a really nice guy. His wife worked days and he worked evenings. He wanted more sex than she did. It seemed like a good arrangement. I was happier for quite a while. I talked to Mark and had sex with Mark. I didn't nag Kel. If he wanted to be a couch potato or go fishing, I didn't care. Pretty soon, though, I didn't care about anything with him. I thought having an outside relationship would make me less of a burden to Kel. In a way I guess it did."

As time went on, Jessica became more distant from Kel and stopped making any effort to be involved with him. It was disturbing to her that the more they were apart the more comfortable he seemed. A year later they divorced. She says, "When I started to see what even a minimal relationship could be, I realized Kel and I had nothing worth saving." The idea

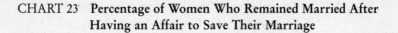

CHART 23 **Percentage of Women Who Remained Married After Having an Affair to Save Their Marriage**

Wolfe, 1975

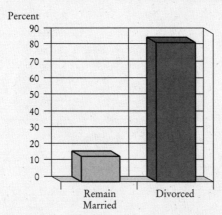

Only 3 of the 21 women studied remained married five years after they had an affair to save their marriage.

that women can subsidize an ailing marriage with an affair seldom works out. The contrast with a more caring relationship, in fact, makes the marriage unbearable.

▼ WOMEN ARE MORE LIKELY TO HAVE SEX DURING OVULATION, BUT . . .

Women are more likely to have intercourse during ovulation with their lover but not with their husband. Bellis and Baker found that there was no pattern to women having sex with their steady partners but that sex on the side peaked at the height of the women's monthly fertility cycles. Several evolutionary psychologists suggest that this willingness of a woman to mate with and bear children with a man other than her husband is a primitive biological drive to keep her gene pool more

CHART 24   **Percentage of Children Fathered by the Mother's Husband or Her Lover in North America**

U.S. News & World Report, July 19, 1993

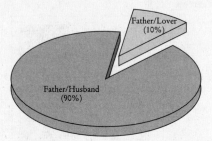

Ten percent of babies born in North America are conceived during extramarital sex.

diverse and healthier and to ensure the woman additional resources should her primary mate disappear.

The sexual drives women feel while they are ovulating can easily lead to unwanted pregnancy. *U.S. News & World Report* states, "Studies of blood typing show that as many as 1 out of every 10 babies born in North America is not the offspring of the mother's husband."

▼ THE DIVORCE RATE IS HIGHER AMONG PEOPLE WHO HAVE AFFAIRS

Spouses who did not have affairs had the lowest rate of divorce, according to Annette Lawson's study of 500 British subjects. Women who had multiple affairs, especially if they started early in the marriage, had the highest rate of divorce.

CHART 25   **Number of Affairs Related to Divorce or Separation**

Lawson, 1988

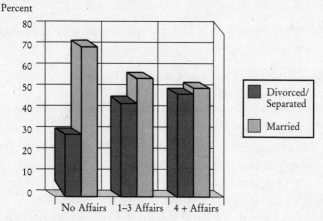

Percent

Legend:
■ Divorced/Separated
■ Married

Categories: No Affairs | 1–3 Affairs | 4 + Affairs

People who have several affairs have a higher divorce rate.

People who have affairs do put their marriage at risk even though many profess that the affair is about themselves or helps their marriage. The evidence does not support the idea that affairs stabilize marriages.

For some the desire for a new mate is compelling—and seemingly irresistible. It is also very risky!

While both men and women engage in extramarital sex in nearly equal numbers, women have more requirements before they engage in intercourse. A study at the University of Hawaii by Elaine Hatfield found that both single men and single women were asked one of the following three questions and the results clearly indicate the difference in the attitude of men and women.

▼ ▬▬▬▬▬▬▬▬▬▬▬▬▬▬▬▬▬▬▬▬▬▬

1. **Would you go on a date with me tonight?**
   Women: 50% Yes   *Men*: 50% Yes

2. **Would you go back to my apartment with me tonight?**
   Women: 6% Yes   *Men:* 69% Yes

3. **Would you have sex with me tonight?**
   Women: 0% Yes   *Men:* 75% Yes

▬▬▬▬▬▬▬▬▬▬▬▬▬▬▬▬▬▬▬▬▬▬▬▬

This study suggests that men are more willing to have sex than to have an emotional relationship even if it is only a date. In a survey of marital happiness, nearly 75% of happily married men admitted to a desire for extramarital intercourse while only 27% of women acknowledged that desire.

Men and women have different beliefs and attitudes about sex. Three-quarters of women who have affairs are involved for emotional reasons while only half of the men consider themselves motivated (to some degree) by emotion.

▼ SUMMARY

"Women give sex to get love and men give love to get sex."
—UNKNOWN

A review of history makes it clear that infidelity has been the norm in the behavior of married people and has not changed in modern society. None of the men surveyed who had affairs during the first couple of years of marriage remained faithful later in their married life. The only significant difference between our ancestors and us is that birth control has allowed women to have affairs without becoming pregnant.

Men and women both opt for multiple sex partners if they have the chance. However, the obvious motivation for men's affairs is very different than for women.

There is overwhelming evidence that men desire and have casual sex simply for the pleasure of sex. Men admit that they profess more love and caring than they really feel as a way of engaging women in intercourse. Nearly all women report they have at some time been led to believe a man cared more for them than he did as a way to persuade them to have sex. When women have casual sex it is usually a pathway to emotional intimacy. For many women, it is a backup plan because she is feeling uncertain about her marriage.

Men and women are different in primary reasons they have affairs but the needs men and women have for sex and for love overlap. Both men and women long for acceptance and appreciation; to be understood, enjoyed and loved. The drives that push men and women into affairs are complex and long-standing but they are no longer a mystery.

PART 2

The Needs and Drives That Prompt Affairs

► 5

The Physiology and Psychology of Affairs

Two major forces are at work to promote our attraction to one another: physiological drives and psychological needs. These drives and needs have been amazingly similar from culture to culture throughout human history. The concept of a physiologically based drive to seek new sexual partners has become widely accepted in the last decade. Michael Liebowitz, M.D., first described this complex physiology in his book *The Chemistry of Love* in 1983. He believed that much of human sexual behavior was determined by chemical interactions taking place in the brain, which are separate from cognitive or intellectual functions.

Psychological needs, as originally identified by Abraham Maslow, Ph.D., are those needs that have to be met for a person to thrive. Maslow believed these needs were hierarchical, meaning that the most basic needs had to be met before higher level needs became compelling. He thought the power of unmet needs created an overwhelming drive.

The chemistry of love and the tremendous force of psychological drives are usually described by people having affairs. Being aware of these physiological drives and psychological needs is important in understanding affairs.

▼ THE PHYSIOLOGY OF LOVE

Recent advances in science provide at least part of the answer to the question of why people have found sexual fidelity difficult to maintain in marriage. Studying the physiology of the brain led scientists to identify phenylethylamine (PEA), an amphetamine-type hormone that gives us an "in love" high or sense of romantic love. PEA and other neurochemicals, such as norepinephrine and dopamine, stimulate the brain and create the sense of euphoria, excitement, sleeplessness and giddiness associated with being "in love."

Dr. Liebowitz reports that PEA is always present in the brain in small doses. When a desirable new mate appears, there is an increase in the amount of PEA released by the pituitary gland. PEA is also secreted in increased amounts during extremely stressful or thrilling situations like skydiving or bungee jumping. The extra shot of PEA creates the feeling of exhilaration.

The body's defense mechanisms react to the overproduction of PEA and the body then begins to produce less and less. While there are excessive levels of PEA in the brain, lovers are on natural speed. No wonder lovers can't eat, sleep or talk in complete sentences. As the amount of amphetamines in the brain begins to overflow, the brain signals the body to stop production and calls for calming agents, endorphins. Endorphins now bathe the brain, creating quiet calm and allowing the lovers to return to a normal life of eating, sleeping and conversation.

As the level of PEA falls, the sense of romantic love is over. The PEA high can last for days, weeks or months. It averages about two years and rarely persists for longer than three or four years.

Even the nose is involved in selecting lovers. Pheromone receptors, known as vomeronasal organs (VNO), pick up the scent of sex hormones. Scientists have shown that a woman is most attracted to a man whose smell is the opposite of hers. This varied scent indicates a difference in the couple's immune systems. The immune system of each parent is passed from generation to generation. An immune system that provides the greatest range of resistance to disease gives the child the best chance of survival.

Geneticists even advise that if your lover's odor reminds you of your father or brother, you should have genetic testing before having a child because the incidence of inherited defects and disorders is higher when mates and relatives smell alike.

ROMANTIC LOVE

Romantic love was first described by Vatsyayana in Sanskrit sometime between the first and sixth century A.D. His collection of writings, known as *Kama Sutra*, remains a classic description of romantic love and sexual pleasure.

More recently, William Jankoviak and Edward Fisher studied the vocabulary of 168 cultures to determine if they had words for romantic love. Not surprisingly, 144, or 87%, of these cultures had words in their vocabulary indicating the existence of these feelings among their people.

Romantic love is quick to come and quick to go regardless of our determination to hold on to it. Anthropologist Helen Fisher muses in her book *Anatomy of Love*, "Why does love ebb and flow? The pulse of infatuation, like many of our courting gestures, may be part of nature's scheme—soft wired in the brain by time, by evolution and by ancient patterns of human

CHART 26   Percentage of World Cultures That Have
Words For Romantic Love

Jankoviak & Fisher, 1992

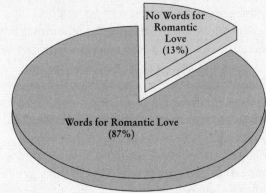

No Words for
Romantic
Love
(13%)

Words for Romantic Love
(87%)

Currently and historically, romantic love is an emotion acknowledged by most societies.

bonding." Familiarity and time bring an end to romantic love.

Romantic love propels people in and out of marriages and in and out of affairs. Sociologists define marriage as an institution created to ensure child-rearing and transfer of property, and around the world many seek romance and sexual pleasure in extramarital affairs.

LASTING LOVE

Of course, many people love one another for more than a few years. Again, the answer lies in the chemistry of the brain. After PEA has returned to normal levels, many people generate another chemical, oxytocin, which is an endorphin. It helps calm the mind and reduces the sense of pain or fear. Oxytocin, "the cuddle chemical," is produced by the pituitary gland and is present in higher levels in people who have long-term love relationships than those who do not have lasting love.

Oxytocin sensitizes nerves and stimulates muscle contractions, enhancing orgasms in both men and women. It creates a feeling of attachment and security.

When we choose to love our spouse and practice a loving attitude and loving behavior we create lasting love. This analysis is not very romantic, but these discoveries provide a biological framework for understanding the feeling of being "in love" and the drives that propel people into marriage—and into affairs. In short:

▶ The feeling of being "in love" is wonderful and not lasting.

▶ Love is a verb, not a noun.

▶ Lasting love is a choice, a decision and an attitude that come from within you.

Lasting love is more than a feeling. It requires care, discipline, attentiveness and skill to survive a lifetime.

▼

The Physiology and the Psychology That Drive Us to Mate and to Marry. . . and Often to Mate Again with a New Partner

Imprinting—Genes and psychological experiences create innate drives to mate.

Feeling in Love—Phenylethylamine, dopamine and norepinephrine are natural amphetamines produced in the brain that create the "in love" feeling.

Attachment—Endorphins are produced in larger quantity, giving lovers a feeling of attachment.

Bonding—Oxytocin, "the cuddle chemical," is an endorphin produced by the pituitary gland that stimulates orgasms and creates a sense of security.

PHYSICAL ATTRACTIVENESS AND AMBITION

David Buss, in an extensive study of 10,000 people in thirty-seven cultures, found that men consistently value physical attractiveness and youth in a mate, while women choose wealth and ambition.

Around the world, the same physical qualities in a woman are considered beautiful. Qualities ranging from clear skin to shiny hair are signs of good physical health. Beyond these features, psychologist Devendra Singh determined that the waist-to-hip ratio men find most desirable (0.67 to 0.80) is the same worldwide and is, in fact, indicative of a woman's fertility. A waist-to-hip ratio around .70 reflects a hormonal balance that distributes weight more to the hips than to the waist, which is linked to greater fertility and a higher resistance to disease. An analysis of *Playboy* centerfolds and beauty contest winners shows that while these women have gotten thinner over the last three decades their waist-to-hip ratio has not changed and is exactly 0.70.

Women, on the other hand, place a higher value on their prospective mate's ambition, status and resources. Physical characteristics such as strength and health are important but rank behind economic capacity.

The qualities men and women choose in a mate are those linked to ensuring the birth of healthy babies from the mother and adequate resources from the father to provide for the child. Dr. Buss says that innate drives honed over thousands of years of evolution motivate us to love and to mate. He explains that infidelity is a deeply rooted part of the human mating strategy, creating more genetic diversity and survival opportunities for humankind. In his 1994 book, *The Evolution of Desire*, he asserts that women want a mate with good economic resources, high social status, a man older than herself with a proven drive for success. He must also be dependable, emotionally stable, compatible with her—plus intelligent! Men opt for women with youth, physical beauty and a particular body shape.

The most "attractive" people in every culture have the highest number of sexual partners. Women find men most attractive if they can provide maximum resources for themselves and their offspring, while men choose women who are healthy and able to bear several children. Sex attracts men and women to one another but it is the emotional ties that bind them together, offering their children the best chance of survival and prosperity.

Women are far more demanding of a variety of characteristics in their mates than men—largely because women are more adversely affected by a mate's reckless behavior or potential abandonment than are men.

Infidelity is part of the primitive drive that pushes both men and women to seek new sexual partners even when they are happily married.

> "Men are most disturbed by sexual infidelity in their mates; a result of uncertainty about paternity. Women are more disturbed by emotional infidelity, because they risk losing their mate's time and resources."
> —WILLIAM ALLMAN, *U.S. NEWS & WORLD REPORT*, 1993

▼ PSYCHOLOGICAL NEEDS

Physiological needs include food, water and oxygen. Psychological needs are primarily emotional, intellectual or interpersonal. They include safety needs, which are security, stability, structure, law and order. Other *Psychological* needs include the need to belong, or to be associated with other people. We need to love and be loved and to have a sense of caring and affection for others. *Self-esteem* needs include feelings of respect, achievement and appreciation. *Self-actualization* means going beyond the self for the well-being of others and does not develop until late in life. *Cognitive* needs involve the desire to know, learn, explore and create. *Aesthetic* needs include the appreciation of art and beauty.

Hierarchy of Needs

Physiological Needs—Oxygen, water, food, minerals, vitamins, livable climate

Safety Needs—Security, stability, dependency, protection, law and order

Belonging Needs—Relations with people, being a member of a group, having friends

To Love and Be Loved—Giving and receiving affection, intimacy and sexuality

Aesthetic Needs—Beauty, sensuality, sensitivity to art

Cognitive Needs—To know and to understand, curiosity, creativity

Self-actualization—Ego-transcendence, openness, humor, altruism, love, individuality

Self-esteem—Respect, satisfaction, mastery, achievement, freedom, dignity

Dr. Maslow postulated that needs are hierarchical. He states, "A person who is lacking food, safety, love and self-esteem would most probably hunger for food more strongly than for anything else." Physiological needs take precedence over all others, and once these needs are satisfied, additional ones emerge. Each time a set of needs are satisfied, new needs become visible—and commanding.

Needs play a role in marriages and affairs because they push people to make choices that are intellectually unreasonable. Self-esteem needs are frequently the motivation for affairs. Partners in marriages that have evolved over the years are subject to criticism, disappointment and struggle. Knowing one another's failures, mistakes and idiosyncrasies can lead to mutual depreciation, weakening or destroying self-esteem.

Lovers seek a sense of understanding based on respect and appreciation for one another. Maslow says, "Satisfaction of the self-esteem needs leads to feelings of confidence, self-worth, strength, capability and adequacy, of being useful and necessary in the world. But thwarting of these needs produces feelings of inferiority, of weakness and of helplessness."

Consider the difference in the relationships Andy has with his wife, Felicia, and his lover, Dana. Felicia says, "Andy used to be a lot of fun. Now he is so passive. He never seems to see what has to be done around the house. He won't make any decisions. He won't even choose a movie. It's always 'I don't care' or 'Whatever you think.' I do everything and make all the decisions or nothing happens."

Dana describes Andy very differently: "Andy is such a great guy. He is a blast to hang with. He makes everything fun. He is so open about his feelings and his thoughts. I never knew a man could be such a good communicator."

Andy and Felicia have a passive-aggressive style in their relationship. Each denies the other the affirmation and appreciation they both need. Andy believes Felicia will criticize everything he does so he tries to avoid conflict by not doing anything and he becomes more and more passive.

Felicia feels frustrated and angry. She is unable to engage Andy as an active partner so she feels alienated and alone. Her needs to belong and to love and be loved are not met.

Dana experiences Andy as fun, confident and talkative. She likes talking to him and she does not have to rely on him to make decisions or contribute to running a household.

Andy says, "At home I feel like the guy who doesn't ever do enough and who is the brunt of the joke. If I say something Felicia doesn't agree with, she rolls her eyes and makes a sarcastic remark.

"When I am with Dana, I feel important. She asks for my advice, she appreciates my work and is interested in what I think. I can tell her anything, about my successes as well as my mistakes. She is never harsh and she never makes fun of me or my quirks."

While Felicia and Andy are unable to give each other a sense of belonging or of being special, Dana and Andy easily meet those needs for one another.

Andy and Felicia have reached a stalemate. They have developed a pattern of neutralizing one another rather than meeting each other's needs. Dana is able to meet several of Andy's self-esteem needs because of the simplicity and single focus of their relationship.

After Felicia and Andy understood how their style of relating to one another left them both feeling helpless and powerless, they began to build a loving and affirming marriage.

There are a few people who pursue one lover after another. They are obsessed with sex and consumed by the desire for new partners, but most people are not promiscuous. Generally, people who have ongoing affairs develop an emotional attachment with the hope of meeting psychological needs. Most people do not intend to have affairs nor do they take pride in their affairs.

"A satisfied need is never a motivator."
—ABRAHAM MASLOW, 1953

NEEDS OR WANTS

While needs are essential human requirements, wants are desires to have more than the usual. For example, self-esteem needs are met by recognition or appreciation for a job well done, a meal well prepared or extra time taken to help someone else. When *things* are the reward for working hard or having a bad day, needs go unmet. There is no end to the number of things a person can want, and no matter how many things one acquires, the needs are no closer to being met.

Acquisitions in the form of possessions, money, knowledge or status get in the way of meeting our needs when they are substituted for interpersonal interactions. Things do not meet needs; they are a distraction from both needs and feelings and they easily undermine relationships. *The major distinction between wants and needs is that needs are satisfiable—wants are unending.*

Like many young couples, Victor and Nadine started out as poor students. They didn't have much money or much stuff but they had each other's full attention. They created good times, which were free.

Victor explains, "When we started out we didn't have much money. We spent hours together, riding bikes, walking around the lake, or just hanging out, talking, laughing and making love. We loved and appreciated one another. I guess we met each other's needs.

"Now we are always shopping for something. We have bought two houses in the last ten years, decorating and furnishing each. It is not all Nadine's fault. I wanted a sound system, she wanted a dining room table, I wanted a billiard table. It seems like all we talk about is what to buy next. I spend more and more time at work. I feel good about myself at work, better than I do at home, plus we need the money."

Now, fourteen years into their marriage, Victor and Nadine spend most of their time and energy acquiring or taking care of their things. Both know something is missing in their marriage but neither has realized that by pursuing their wants they are neglecting their needs.

This acquisitive pattern leaves their marriage very vulnerable to an affair. Sooner or later both Victor and Nadine will feel compelled to meet their needs for intimacy. They will want someone to love and appreciate them for who they are, not what they own.

It is easier to limit wants than to continually struggle to feed them.

▶ 6

Types of Affairs and the Needs They Meet

▼ LOVE AFFAIRS AND SEX AFFAIRS

**Self-esteem needs are the reason given for many affairs.
Self-esteem needs are met through knowing, understanding and acceptance. Self-esteem is enhanced through talking intimately about feelings, thoughts and needs. When we inquire warmly and affirm each other, we meet one another's self-esteem needs.**

There are several types of affairs—and each has different motives, different behaviors, different feelings and different consequences.

The two main categories of affairs are love (emotional) affairs and sex (physical) affairs. They are divided into these categories to help you distinguish between them, develop a better understanding of how and why they happen and know what to do if they do happen.

Love affair   An emotionally and sexually intimate bond between a married person and someone who is not his or her spouse.

Sex affair A liaison between a married person and someone other than his or her spouse that involves genital contact, with little or no emotional involvement.

The feelings evoked by an affair allow diagnosis of its type. The needs met by an affair indicate its motivation, its probable duration and the degree of threat it presents to the marriage. This knowledge allows couples to relate to one another in ways that meet one another's needs and either prevent or undermine an affair.

Needs Met by Affairs

- Being loved
- Being needed
- Being understood
- Enjoyable risk
- Freedom/independence
- Friendship
- Fun
- Intellectual stimulation
- Loving
- Sexual fulfillment

—Lawson

▼ LOVE AFFAIRS

Love affairs have a strong emotional emphasis. They are emotionally intense and are usually sexually intimate also. They may begin as "just talking" and "just having a good time together" and evolve into a powerful bond. Love affairs end in pain and devastation for someone. The reasons given for love affairs are usually related to self-esteem. There are four categories of love affairs: *in-love affairs, loving affairs, bridge affairs* and *hate affairs.*

IN-LOVE AFFAIRS

In-love affairs occur when the amphetamine high from an increased level of PEA drives the lovers beyond reason into a blind passion. This is the kind of love the hero dies for in the movies, risking fame, fortune, everything for "true love." Presumably, the Duke of Windsor gave up the crown of England because he was "in love."

In-love affairs are often reckless, unrealistic, compelling, obsessive, intense and passionate. The lovers feel pain and agony in the absence of one another and euphoria when they are together.

In-love affairs compete directly with a marriage and even replace the marital relationship. In-love affairs are stimulated by biological mating drives that are experienced both physically and emotionally. This intense obsession lasts anywhere from a few weeks to a maximum of two to four years, but it does end.

Jack had created a nice life for himself and his family. He had always been very logical, practical and disciplined until Tammy joined his law firm. The first time he saw her he was overwhelmed by the strength of his desire for her.

Jack is having an in-love affair with Tammy. The magnitude and intensity of his feelings are both disturbing and arousing to him. He feels passion, pain, joy, desire, jealousy, euphoria and ecstasy. He has a sense of connection to her that he has not experienced before. He thinks of her as his soul mate. Realistically he does not know her very well since they only met six months ago, but he believes they intuitively know, understand and accept one another.

The sad thing about in-love affairs is the high price that is paid when a family crumbles, only to have the feelings that drove the decision change. The lovers later find they do not know each other as well as they imagined and they are usually not as compatible as they hoped.

LOVING AFFAIRS

Loving affairs are usually based on friendship, caring and understanding and are a refuge from the duties, pressures and responsibilities of day-to-day life. They are predominantly emotional and may or may not have a sexual component. They offer opportunity for self-discovery, sex, experimentation, counseling and acceptance.

The affairee is a confidant(e) and friend. Affairees feel love and caring for one another but do not seriously consider leaving their spouses. Loving affairs last years, decades—and even a lifetime!

If discovered, loving affairs are temporarily suspended but resumed later. Affairees believe loving affairs enhance their marriages by meeting their needs.

Bonnie and Steve worked together for seven years before they became lovers. They are close friends. They trust and admire one another. They do not profess undying love or passion. In fact, they joke that they could never live with each other because, as Steve says, "I love how organized and meticulous Bonnie is but having to have everything perfect at home would drive me nuts."

Bonnie and Steve both believe their loving affair helps their marriages by making them more satisfied with themselves and their lives. They are tender, caring and respectful of one another.

They give each other accurate feedback and help one another through difficult times. They believe they work well together because they have a deep understanding and respect for one another.

BRIDGE AFFAIRS

Bridge affairs occur during transitions. They happen between people who want casual, fun and ego-enhancing experiences. They are likely to occur during positive transitions such as a promotion, award, the spouse starting a new or better job, the birth of a child or a move to a new home. Often with success there is a new sense of competence and a desire for a special reward, to be with someone who is appreciative, easy to please and fun.

Bridge affairs also occur during bad times, when the affairee wants someone who will support, comfort and understand the affairee's failure, disappointment and distress.

Bridge affairs are short-lived, lasting less than a year, and seldom disrupt the marriage. Only a few are discovered.

Tim says, "It had been a good year for me and a hard year for my wife, Elizabeth. She lost her job in layoffs and it took her six months to find another one. During that same time one or the other of our kids had ear infections most of the time. Elizabeth was pretty crabby but I knew she was having a hard time. I didn't take it personally.

"I met Anna during a conference. It was great just to relax and joke with her. She has a great sense of humor. The sex was easy. We both wanted it.

"I see Anna once in a while, maybe once a month; we always have a good time. Being with Anna takes some of the pressure off my marriage."

Needs

Safety—sense of options and choices
Sense of belonging—sense of inclusion
Love and be loved—sense of acceptance
Self-esteem—sense of appreciation

Feelings

Appreciation, acceptance, security, optimism, joy, worry, guilt

Tim's relationship with Anna is superficial but it gives him a sense of security. Believing he can have a relationship with her makes him feel confident that he has options other than with Elizabeth.

Elizabeth has been struggling with her new job and sick kids and has not had much energy to put into her marriage. Tim chooses to meet his needs outside the marriage rather than negotiate with Elizabeth. In fact, he believes he is doing Elizabeth a favor by not asking more of her.

HATE AFFAIRS

Some women hate men and some men hate women. They find pleasure in hurting, deceiving and manipulating other people. They lie easily and well.

They need to dominate. They choose people who are vulnerable or innocent. They promise everything and deliver pain, disappointment and humiliation refreshed with new promises and apologies.

The affairee is usually smooth in approach, which can range from playing a flamboyantly successful person to a pathetic victim who would get better "if only someone understood."

They start by pumping up their affairee, then they gradually disappoint, frustrate, subjugate and manipulate their partner. They take money, time, energy and self-esteem from their lover. They do not leave their spouse.

Crystal and John's affair is typical of this destructive situation. As Crystal says, "I was in awe of John. He is tall, good-looking and very charming. Of course, I knew he was married. Guys like him are always married.

"When he looked deep into my eyes, I felt like he was looking into my soul. He said I was the most beautiful woman he had ever met. No one had ever talked to me the way he did. I fell in love with him.

"He was having a hard time with his business. Sometimes he had to stay and work late, so he would have to break our date. Other times we would plan to meet at a restaurant or a movie, but he wouldn't show up—no excuses! I did things for him I am ashamed of—I even loaned him money. I was so much in love I could not see what was happening. A friend of mine said he was a misogynist, a man who hates women. Maybe she was right."

Needs

Safety—a sense of control through domination

Feelings

Fear, domination, exhilaration, disappointment, anticipation, enthusiasm, distrust, puzzlement, humiliation, desperation, despair

Crystal had never been popular with men. She was a bit timid and self-deprecating. She could hardly believe it when John invited her to dinner. She worried because he was married, but no one like John had even talked to her before. She rationalized that it was only dinner.

At first John's demands appealed to her. His insistence on seeing her and having sex with her made her feel needed. While she felt puzzled and apprehensive she also felt safe with John because she believed she was helping him.

People like John are filled with hate and have no guilt or remorse about using or damaging other people. John belittled, humiliated and bilked Crystal of $20,000 before he abandoned her.

▼ SEX AFFAIRS

Sex affairs involve genital contact between a married person and another who is not their spouse. They are basically physical, with little or no emotional involvement. There are three types of sex affairs: *sensual affairs, sexual adventure affairs* and *sexual conquest affairs.*

SENSUAL AFFAIRS

Sensual affairs are primarily sexual but with a sensitivity to the physical pleasure of one another. The affairees care about one another and like one another, although not much time is spent talking. They experiment with everything from massage oils to whipped cream.

If they can find a new position or play a new game, they are delighted. They have fun together and enjoy the passion of the moment. Sensual affairees believe these affairs are unrelated to their relationship with their spouse or that the affair has a positive impact on their marriage. Their physical relationship can span decades but they never shared day-to-day life. One of the main reasons sensual affairs are long-lasting is that they are emotionally positive with no demands.

Jake boasts, "I have always liked sex and I worried before I got married whether I could be satisfied with one lover. I wasn't. I think about sex all the time. I enjoy intercourse but I really love touching, exploring and teasing my lover. I can spend long hours making love in the grass, on my desk, in the hot tub. Wherever and whenever.

"My lover is Toby. She has an incredible body and she is willing to try anything. We have been lovers and friends for seven years. We don't know much about one another's lives but we know every inch of each other's body."

Needs

Self-esteem—a sense of acceptance

Feelings

Arousal, excitement, fantasy, tenderness, thrill, pleasure, eroticism, mischievousness, delight, desire, devilishness

SEXUAL ADVENTURE AFFAIRS

Sexual adventure affairs are physical. They are usually for sport and may be driven by challenge, experimentation or rebellion. Adventure affairs are playful, secretive and naughty. The affairees often feel like children with a new toy that belongs to someone else.

The affairees are self-oriented, seeking their own pleasure and experience in the present. Their affairs may recur but without much regularity. The greatest dangers they present are health risks related to sexually transmitted diseases, including AIDS, because of the high number of sexual partners they have.

For adventurers, sex is simply a game of challenge, control and conquest. For Cal, the more lovers he could "have," the more important he felt. He especially wanted those who weren't easily available. He liked the chase and relished the conquest.

Cal grins as he recalls, "I knew Jeri when we were in college but we never dated. We both married. I knew the guy she married; we were in the same fraternity. She is one of the sexiest women I have ever seen.

"We were at a meeting together and I decided to see if she was sexually available. At first she resisted, saying she would never cheat.

"I convinced her after a few drinks that a little sport sex was not cheating and no one would ever know. She argued but she was intrigued. Finally, I won and we spent a great evening in bed."

Jeri had always been a "good girl," loyal, honest, sincere and stable. She said, "I was sick of being so good. I was bored with my perfect little life. When Cal started coming on to me at the conference, I first found myself amused, then curious. He had always been a 'bad boy' in college. He was persistent and flattering. Finally I thought, 'What the hell—for once I'm going to be naughty.' Afterward I felt sneaky and silly but it just wasn't that big a deal."

Needs

Self-esteem—a sense of competence

Feelings

Competition, challenge, excitement, naughtiness, and cleverness

Sexual Conquest Affairs

Some affairs are literally one-night stands. There is no emotional relationship and often the affairee's name is either not known or not remembered.

The affairees are usually trying to prove something, and they are motivated toward their own gratification. The basis of their need to pursue repeated impersonal sexual encounters can be a manifestation of self-doubt, rebellion, anger or retaliation.

Sexual conquest affairs are rarely discovered or confessed.

Multiple sex affairs may be a symptom of deep emotional pain and dysfunction.

Mariah didn't like or understand other women. She viewed herself as in constant competition with them. She had never been able to develop anything more than casual friendships. She viewed men as things belonging to other women. If she could get someone's husband into bed she thought she was as good as they were.

Mariah describes herself, "I have never been very popular. I am nice to people, but a lot of women are snobs. They treat me like a second-class citizen. Maybe I don't make as much money, but I can have any one of their husbands whenever I want. If they snub me, sometimes I intentionally go after one of their husbands, just to prove they are no better than I am.

"I have a slogan, 'I always get my man!' Sometimes, I hint at the intimacy I have with a husband. You should see these women squirm."

Needs

Self-esteem—a sense of power combined with self-doubt

Feelings

Desire, pride, relief, regret, hostility, loneliness, superiority, disdain, revenge, retaliation

▼ When Men Have Love Affairs Rather Than Sex Affairs

Early in marriage men seek sex affairs rather than love affairs. The primary motivation is physical pleasure, challenge or experience. A few are keeping score and will readily confess to having hundreds or even a thousand partners.

As time goes on, a higher percentage of men become involved in love affairs, where they experience an emotional as well as a sexual bond. They want to talk to someone who understands them, who accepts them and who appreciates them for who they are and what they have accomplished.

CHART 27   Percentage of Men's Love Affairs or Sex Affairs
              Related to Years of Marriage

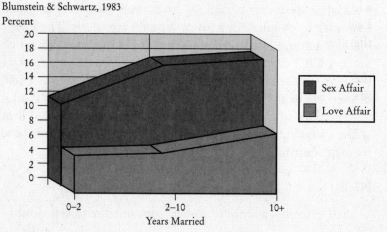

Blumstein & Schwartz, 1983

Husbands are more likely to have affairs after 10 years of marriage.

CHART 28 **Percentage of Women's Love Affairs or Sex Affairs Related to Years of Marriage**

Blumstein & Schwartz, 1983

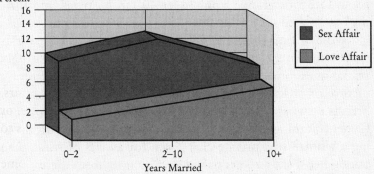

Wives are more likely to have affairs after 10 years of marriage.

▼ WHEN WOMEN HAVE LOVE AFFAIRS RATHER THAN SEX AFFAIRS

The longer a woman is married, the more likely she is to have a love affair. Women have love affairs to meet emotional needs. Loneliness is the feeling that many women believe motivated them to have an affair.

Women choose sex affairs for fun, sexual experience and the opportunity to experiment. Occasionally women choose sex affairs for revenge and out of anger and fear.

▼ CYBERAFFAIRS

A cyberaffair is an intimate or sexually explicit communication between a married person and someone other than their spouse that takes place on the computer over the Internet. This communication requires that both parties subscribe to an on-line service such as America On-Line or CompuServe. About

25 million people access the Internet, so the chances of meeting someone over the Net are very high. You simply select the category of "chat room" you would like to visit. The chat room categories range from "over 40" to "married and flirting" to "naked on the keyboard."

Women find that after a little conversation that is flirtatious but seems benign, they are confronted with increasingly sexual questions and comments. Men may ask a woman for a picture or at least her profile. They may ask the size of her breasts or what kind of sex she likes. They ask, "Are you into Cyber (meaning cybersex)?" Some men are more subtle, inviting a woman to a private chat room for a glass of wine, then asking her if she will get naked—and it goes from there.

Men usually demand a phone number with the hope that they can talk women into a real-life affair. By far the majority of cyberaffairs are sexually graphic and often crude.

Affairs over the Internet differ from physical world affairs. Cyberaffairs are based on written communication where people often feel freer to express themselves anonymously than they would in person. They will tell their life stories, reveal their innermost secrets and divulge their wildest fantasies.

Men are less shy about exploring and expressing their feelings while on-line than in person. While wives may find husbands reluctant to talk about emotions to them, these same men will, in a cyberaffair, dislodge their inhibitions and write about their fleeting fantasies and impassioned emotions.

Women can become more sexually adventurous and explicit on-line than they would be face to face. For many women it is an opportunity to pretend to be different than they are.

Pretending is a major theme in cyberaffairs. Most men say they are professionals—doctors, lawyers or accountants—and of course they all work out at the gym every day. And, nearly universally, they explain that if their wives liked sex, they wouldn't be sex shopping on the Internet.

The dangers are the same as the opportunities. The desire to explore and express feelings and to be known as you would like to be is engaging but it is easy to begin to believe the fantasy.

Mattie logged on and found a chat room one day just out of curiosity. She recalls, "I was astonished at how many men came on within a few minutes and wanted to know me. I thought it would be fun to make some new friends. It was hard at first to learn the language of cyberland but I was surprised at how fast I got witty and playful with people I didn't know. Boy, was I naive. The flirting was fun—to have all these guys, five or six at a time, who wanted to talk to me. It was very flattering.

"When men asked me questions I told the truth. I even gave one guy my phone number. I thought we were all telling the truth but it soon became clear that wasn't the case. I got sucked into answering questions about myself and what I liked sexually that I never would have told anyone in person.

"Every chance I had, I would go on-line and see who was there. You have a code name—mine was Topper. There is a buddy list so when I came on-line if I was on someone's buddy list they would receive a message that I was on. I spent hours. It was a thrill.

"I began to realize I was addicted. If I wasn't on-line I was thinking about it. Every spare moment I had, I was on-line, even staying up late.

"I started to get scared as the instant messages sent specifically to me became more aggressive. For instance, one guy wrote, 'Take your clothes off, now, right now. Touch your breasts and tell me how they feel,' and so forth. That was bad enough but even though I was scared I kept going back.

"Then while my teenage daughter and her boyfriend were on the Internet a picture of a nude man masturbating came on the screen asking for me to help him. My daughter thought it was funny. I didn't. I was mortified.

"I don't go to chat rooms anymore but some of these guys still find me anytime I'm on the Internet. It is really intimidating."

Sometimes emotionally intimate relationships do develop. Polly fell in love on the Net. She started talking to Daryl about six months before they met. She says, "I was in love. I thought about Daryl all the time. I compared the way he wanted to talk to me and understand me to the way my husband treated me. Even though my husband is nice to me, he certainly wasn't as attentive or flattering as Daryl. Daryl wanted me and I knew it.

"Daryl said he was lonely. His wife had cancer so they could no longer be lovers. He said he was a little overweight and a bit bald. He sounded real. I had to meet Daryl.

"I told my husband I was not happy and wanted some time for myself. I went to meet Daryl. Daryl was overweight and bald but charming and attentive. We made love the first day we met. I felt like I have known him forever. I spent a week in a hotel near his office and he came to see me every day and most evenings. After about five days I began to realize this was just an affair. I had put everything at risk, my marriage, my family and myself for an affair with a man I didn't know. I don't even know whether his wife really had cancer.

"I went back home shaken and scared. I recommitted to my marriage and I am off the Internet—for good."

Cyberaffairs are better than real relationships can ever be. No one in cyberland has bad breath, dirty hair or body odor, ever! And sex, the best you can imagine! Sex is giving, loving, sensual, erotic, selfless, gentle, rough, tender—whatever you want, whenever you want it and just the way you want it.

In cyberland men are warm, sensitive, understanding and communicative and women are adventurous, daring, playful and hungry for wild, erotic sex. The fantasy lover wants to understand you and appreciates you and desires to know every inch of your being. Too good to be true? Yes. Remember it is only make-believe.

When cyberlovers meet, the letdown is inevitable. No real person can compete with a dream lover and no marriage can compete with a cyberaffair when it comes to adventure, dramatic revelations and safe self-expression. But no cyberaffair can compete with a healthy marriage for intimacy, companionship, friendship and making love.

▼ SUMMARY

Amphetamines and endorphins are designated to create the feeling of love and the drive to mate. This complex physiology and psychology binds men and women together long enough to produce a child and nurture it through its most vulnerable years. Then the chemistry is altered and the psychological needs shift and both men and women are ready to mate again.

It is abundantly clear from the research that men have affairs for sex and are willing to lie, cheat and manipulate to that end. Women are no less corrupt or driven to develop emotional bonds.

A combination of these biological drives and emotional needs is what I hear in explanations of affairs. The needs and drives that propel a person into an affair are real, and the feelings, while temporary, are intense.

While there are many different types of affairs, usually the main purpose of an affair is physical and emotional attention.

An affair does not meet the same needs that a marriage meets. The needs met by the marriage are difficult to identify because they are being satisfied. The most commanding needs are those that are unmet.

It is love affairs that present the greatest danger to a marriage. Self-esteem needs are the motivation for love affairs. Spouses often neglect one another's self-esteem needs; lovers don't. Self-esteem needs are met through knowing and understanding each other and expressing our acceptance with compliments, an appreciative nod, a loving smile or an affectionate caress.

"Love is strongest in pursuit, friendship in possession."
—RALPH WALDO EMERSON

Most affairs do not last more than a few years, but some of the consequences do.

PART 3

Information and Advice for the Affairee

The person involved in an affair has several choices about how to manage the affair. I have included information about the good times as well as the sad times for both affairees.

Affairs can be thrilling, fun, challenging, delightful and ego-enhancing. They provide renewed energy and zest for life. Feelings never felt before, or at least not remembered, become part of everyday life.

Affairees often encourage one another to have new experiences and to understand themselves in new ways. An affair can be a catalyst for an emotional awakening. An affair can provide a person with love, joy and sex as well as a sense of being understood and appreciated.

However, rarely do affairs last forever and seldom do

they become happy marriages. So, sooner or later, regret and pain set in.

I have seen several clients who believed an affair was more than it actually turned out to be, or encountered consequences they never would have dreamed possible. Feelings and intentions are easily misunderstood by one participant or the other during an affair. Words spoken in the heat of passion can be heard as promises, and broken promises often become a basis for hatred. These misunderstandings may lead to disaster. Lovers can and do become enemies, often with a vengeance.

While affairees are usually very aware of the needs met by their lover, those met by their spouse often go unrecognized. I have included in this section some feelings and thoughts expressed by both women and men about their lovers.

▸ 7

Costs and Consequences

▼ SEXUALLY TRANSMITTED DISEASES

No one expects to get a sexually transmitted disease but millions do. It can happen to you.

The Surgeon General reports that 25 million Americans are infected with genital herpes. Eight million cases of sexually transmitted diseases (STDs) occur annually among people under 25 years of age. Hepatitis B infects 300,000 adults, causing permanent liver damage and resulting in 5,000 deaths annually.

These diseases are not selective. Everyone—regardless of sexual orientation, age, education, wealth or social prominence—is at risk. *There is no free sex.*

Women's Symptoms of STDs or HIV Infections

- ▸ Vaginal yeast infections (more than three per year)
- ▸ Open sores on genitalia
- ▸ Copious discharge or pungent odor
- ▸ Pelvic infections

▶ Cervical cancer

▶ Tuberculosis

▶ Pneumonia

—Surgeon General, *Report of HIV*, 1993

▼ EXPOSURE TO HIV

The American Association for the Advancement of Science advises, "Heterosexuals should not wait for HIV infection rates to increase dramatically before they take preventive action." The Association's research shows that the lowest rate of exposure to HIV was between 15% and 30% of adult heterosexuals in cities in the Midwest where the incidence of infection was low. The risk of exposure was between 20% and 41% in cities on the East and West Coasts where there is a high incidence of infection.

CHART 29   **Percentage of Heterosexuals Who Risked Exposure to HIV, Related to the Level of Infection in Their City, Between 1987 and 1992**

Science, November 13, 1992

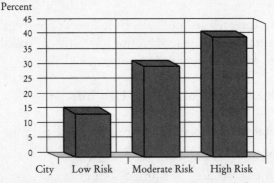

Between 15% and 41% of heterosexual adults risked exposure to HIV in a five-year period.

Only 17% of heterosexual men and women who have multiple sexual partners use condoms every time they have intercourse. More frightening, only 12.6% of those who know that their sexual partners are at risk for HIV infection use condoms every time they have intercourse.

▼ HETEROSEXUALS—WOMEN, MIDDLE-AGED MEN AND OLDER MEN ARE AT RISK

The number of heterosexual women with AIDS has jumped by 25% in the last four years. Women and low income individuals are the most likely heterosexuals to be exposed to HIV. Approximately 71% of those surveyed reported not using condoms.

Middle-aged and older men tend to think the partners they choose would not be HIV infected, even when they know

CHART 30   **Number of Cases Reported of HIV Transmission Through Heterosexual Contact**

Novello, 1993

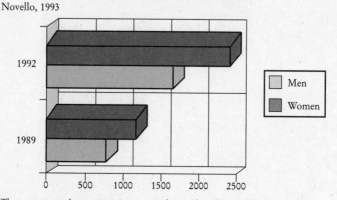

There was more than a 100% increase in the number of cases of heterosexually transmitted HIV in four years.

their lover has other lovers. These men are reluctant to use condoms or to ask their partners to be tested for HIV. This attitude puts everyone at risk.

The Centers for Disease Control warns: *"A woman is at least ten times more susceptible to contracting HIV during intercourse than a man."*

▼ Protection against HIV and STDs

Latex condoms are the only barrier recognized by most researchers to prevent infection by HIV, and condoms are not always effective.

There are a few controversial studies indicating the effectiveness of nonoxynol-9 in killing HIV when used in conjunction with condoms. Nonoxynol-9 is an active ingredient in many spermicides. Considering the ability of HIV to mutate, the success of nonoxynol-9 in stopping HIV is limited, at best.

Latex (NOT lambskin) condoms should be used with a water-based lubricant, such as K-Y Jelly.

► 8

An Affair Is Just an Affair

Affairs are exciting, fulfilling and engulfing. They are also transient!

Affairs meet both physiological and psychological needs. They can add thrills, adventure and excitement to life. The needs that affairs meet in women are different from those met in men. Knowing what an affair is and is not can save disappointment, heartache and even disaster.

The type of affair you are involved in is defined by the needs it meets. Sex affairs are for sexual and sensual pleasure; they are seldom long-term and they do not become love affairs.

Love affairs, such as loving affairs and bridge affairs, can become long-term friendships. In-love affairs are the most powerful and life-altering. The feelings are nearly overwhelming. In-love affairs end in tremendous pain. Despite their depth, in-love feelings change.

Alex and Paula met playing mixed doubles at their tennis

club. Alex remembers, "I could hardly wait to finish the match so I could talk to her. We hit it off instantly. I invited her to lunch and we talked for three hours. I missed two business appointments but I couldn't tear myself away from her.

"I felt like I had always known her. I found myself telling her things I had never told anyone. She was like another part of me. I felt so lost when I wasn't with her. I felt more married to Paula than I did to my wife, Sue.

"I remember telling a friend that I felt married to Paula in spirit and to Sue on paper. I wanted to share everything with Paula—my home, my friends, my daughter."

Paula was head over heels in love with Alex. Paula recalls, "I had never felt very sexual. I had been with several men but I thought sex was overrated until I met Alex. I had never had any feelings of lust or desire until the first time Alex touched me. I couldn't believe myself; I wanted sex—lots of sex. We would talk, touch, then make love. We spent days kissing, talking and making love. I knew, whatever it took, I had to be with Alex. No one else could make me feel this way. He was the one for me."

Compare what Alex and Paula felt at the beginning of their affair and what they think and feel now, four years later, after two years of marriage.

Alex four years ago—"I feel like we are already married. In spirit, we are; all that is missing is a piece of paper. I will do whatever it takes for us to be husband and wife. I want us to have a baby together."

Alex now—"I tore my family apart. I didn't care about anything or anybody else. I couldn't think clearly. I thought about Paula all the time. I didn't believe my feelings would ever change. They did. Now we have a normal life instead of an affair and we don't have much in common, including sex.

We don't even like the same music. I am sick of her competing with my daughter."

Paula four years ago—"I love his passion. He is always touching me and telling me how beautiful I am. I want to make love every day with Alex for the rest of my life."

Paula now—"I feel trapped. He always wants something. He is too sensitive. He thinks about sex all the time. I have other things to do."

Paula and Alex had a good relationship as affairees. They added something to one another's life that was missing—passion. When the passion faded and the affair was over, the marriage did not work for either of them. The very quality that drew them together, their intense sexual desire for one another, later became a major problem. They divorced two years after they married.

▼ WHAT TO EXPECT FROM AN AFFAIR

Affairs meet emotional and physical needs. Pain occurs when they end, and they dissipate in an average of two years. Men and women both report that they consider the affair to be a good experience, although women are less likely than men to want to have another. The primary needs met by affairs are different for women and men.

Expect the affair to be intense, passionate and, perhaps, loving. Don't expect it to become a happy, long-term marriage. It doesn't turn out that way.

Jess thought he had found the perfect woman in Brenda, but look how his feeling changed in one year.

Jess then—"She has an incredible body (36–26–34) and she likes to show it off. She works out every day and I have never seen her in the same outfit twice. She is a knockout. I love watching other men look at her, knowing I have her and they don't. She is so innocent. Everything I do pleases her. She even laughs at my jokes. She is thrilled when we go out. I love her smile, her laugh and her touch."

Jess one year later—"I liked feeling like I knew more than she did; it boosted my ego, I guess. It only took ninety days to get divorced. I was sure Brenda was the right one for me. Now, I'm irritated by her lack of knowledge. She doesn't know about anything. She is silly and tiresome. Her most complicated thought is what she is going to wear. I hate going out. She is always flirting. She spends a fortune on clothes and spends most of her time in front of a mirror. She gives every man the signal she is available. She doesn't discourage anybody."

The same qualities men and women enjoy in their partner during an affair are sources of tension with time. Both men and women require more from a marriage partner than from a lover.

▼
Women—Needs Met by Affair
(in order of importance)

1. Being loved
2. Friendship
3. Sexual fulfillment
4. Loving
5. Fun
6. Being needed
7. Being understood
8. Intellectual stimulation
9. Enjoyable risk
10. Freedom/independence

—Lawson

▼
Men—Needs Met by Affair
(in order of importance)

1. Sexual fulfillment
2. Friendship
3. Being loved
4. Fun
5. Loving
6. Being needed
7. Enjoyable risk
8. Intellectual stimulation
9. Being understood
10. Freedom/Independence

—Lawson

▼ WOMEN'S THOUGHTS ABOUT THEIR AFFAIRS

▶ The affair has positive effects on a woman's marriage because she has a greater sense of autonomy and less resentment toward her husband.

▶ Affairs offer change, variety and risk, while marriages offer predictability and security.

▶ The affair allows more freedom to experiment emotionally and sexually.

▶ The affair allows a woman to meet her expressive needs, as men communicate more in affairs than they do in marriage.

▶ The most negative aspects of the affair are the lack of time and the lying.

Della sighs as she describes her affair with Allan. "Allan is the kind of guy women whisper 'What a hunk' about. He has a great body and he is kind and sensitive. We have a lot of fun, laughing and telling stories. We even play 'doctor.' Silly things.

"He is not anyone I would ever consider marrying, but he is a wonderful friend. He is so different from my husband. Dillon is brilliant; he works long hours. I love Dillon and have immense respect for him.

"I think my affair with Allan makes me more supportive and affectionate with Dillon. I used to get angry with Dillon because he was gone so much. It seemed like his job was more important than me. Now I am happier and our marriage is better. I do feel guilty about lying, and sometimes I'm out with Allan when I could be getting more done at home. I would feel horrible if Dillon ever found out because I think it would hurt him."

Della is clear in her thinking that her affair is just an affair and is entirely different from her marriage. As is often true, married women will have an affair with a man they would not have even dated if they were single.

How Women Feel About Their Lovers

▶ *Caring* is the feeling most women have for their lovers.

▶ Women feel *thrilled* by their lover's interest in them physically, emotionally and intellectually.

▶ An affair is *exciting* for a woman, giving her a chance to know a different man, how he thinks and feels.

▶ Women feel *intimate* with their lovers because they can talk about their feelings openly.

▶ Women feel *loving* with their lovers.

Women make conscious choices about having an affair. Affairs are rarely spur-of-the-moment sexual encounters with a stranger. Women who have affairs know exactly whom they are choosing, why they are choosing that person and how emotionally involved they will get.

Kate chose Sean as a lover because he was younger, sexy and he appreciated her professional accomplishments. She clearly knew what she wanted from Sean. Kate explains, "When I am with Sean I feel so alive. He loves to touch me—everywhere. He wants to know what I think and what I feel. He makes me feel important. He respects my knowledge and asks for my advice.

"We can spend hours in bed talking, laughing and loving one another. I feel free and excited with him. Since he isn't in another relationship, I feel sorry for him because I know he is lonely, particularly during special occasions."

Kate also knows the limits of their relationship, saying, "Sean is a nice guy and I care for him. I feel loving and tender toward him. I'm certainly not 'in love' with him but I help him out professionally and personally when I can."

After two and three years Della and Kate both ended their affairs. Over time both began to feel guilty in relation to their husbands, not so much because of the sex but because of the lying and deceit inherent in hiding the affair. Neither of them wanted to threaten their marriage, and they became increasingly worried that they would be discovered. Kate believed that if her husband found out about the affair it wouldn't hurt the marriage, but she worried about her kids finding out and the message that would send to them.

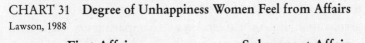

CHART 31   Degree of Unhappiness Women Feel from Affairs
Lawson, 1988

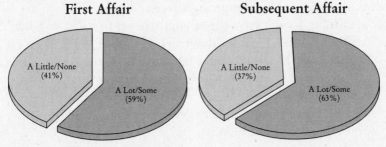

First Affair

A Little/None (41%)

A Lot/Some (59%)

Subsequent Affair

A Little/None (37%)

A Lot/Some (63%)

Reasons Women Have Pain During Affairs
(in order of importance)

1. Guilt in relation to spouse
2. Deceit
3. Fear of being found out
4. Hurt to the marriage
5. Guilt in relation to children
6. Own jealous feelings
7. Other's jealousy

—Lawson

▼ Men's Thoughts About Their Affairs

▸ The affair had no effect on the marriage.

▸ The affair made the marriage easier.

▸ The affair made them more responsive to their wives.

▸ Discovery of the affair made their wives more attentive to them.

▸ The marriage improved after the discovery of an affair.

▸ Men rarely feel guilty for very long.

Men describe themselves as feeling natural in having more than one lover. They think of their marriage as entirely different from an affair. As Warren says, "Comparing my affair with my marriage is like comparing silver and gold. While silver is beautiful it doesn't have the strength, luster or value of gold."

Warren smiles as he describes his affair with Monica: "When I met Monica I could feel her across the room. I was fascinated by her every move; her laughter was mesmerizing; I wanted to be with her. When we danced I could hardly make myself let her go. I called her every few days. I tried to get her off my mind, but I couldn't.

"Eventually, I talked her into seeing me. When we made love, it was incredible. I had never had sex like this before. I love Monica. She has added so much to my life, and I do not want to hurt her, but I will never divorce Jan. She is my wife, the mother of my children, and my friend. I could never leave her. In many ways, I appreciate her more than ever."

Warren's relationship with Monica is compartmentalized in his mind. He views the two relationships as totally separate. He believes that having sex and fun with Monica makes him appreciate Jan even more. He says, "I get more sex with Monica, which leaves me in a better mood, but as much as I love being with her there is no comparison between my love for Monica and my love for Jan. Jan looks after the kids and me. She is smart, conscientious and concerned about other people. I have tremendous love and admiration for her and I am committed to our marriage."

While Warren has a lot of feeling for Monica he has no intention of leaving his marriage. While he does not think he is misleading Monica with his words of love, she is, nevertheless, waiting for him to leave his wife and be her partner.

How Men Feel About Their Lovers

▶ Sex is *exciting* and the most important part of the affair.

▶ It is important that the love feelings are *controlled* in the affair and do not compete with their feelings for their wife.

▶ Men are *careful* to limit their emotional involvement with their lover—intentionally.

▶ Even when *passionate* about their lover, men do not seriously contemplate divorce. Statements like "I love you" or "I have never felt like this before" or "I cannot imagine life without you" do not mean he will leave his wife. Even if he does, he is unlikely to marry his lover.

Frank has had several affairs, which he considers successful. He cares about his partners, and in fact loves them. He has some problems in his marriage and his affairs help him deal with them. He says, "I have always been successful in just about everything I have tried, but in the past few years nothing I did for my wife, Gloria, seemed to be quite right. I remember buying her a very expensive necklace she had admired in the jeweler's window. She returned it, saying it didn't hang right. Whenever I took her to her favorite restaurant, the table was too noisy, the wine too dry and so on. She always had something to complain about.

"Six months later when I took Erica to a simple little restaurant, she was delighted. She was interested in me; she appreciated my thoughtfulness. She seemed to like everything, everywhere we went. The sex is fun and playful. She likes me and I like being with her. It really helps me to not be so sensitive to Gloria, and we get along better."

Frank, like many other men, genuinely cares about his lover. He finds her exciting. He is delighted that he can please her so easily. He dreams of taking her to exotic places or spending a week on a deserted beach making love morning, noon and night. He even talks about living with her in a love nest next to a pristine little lake where he fished as a child. For Frank these are only fantasies.

Erica's perception is very different. She knows Frank isn't happy in his marriage, because he talks about how rejected he feels by Gloria and how hard she is to please. She muses, "Frank is always taking me someplace special or doing something nice for me. He even bought me a sapphire ring. I think he will divorce Gloria when their kids are a little older. We even picked out a piece of property to build a little house on. I can have a garden and Frank can fish. We will probably have a place in the city, too, but the cottage on the lake near where he grew up will be our love nest. When we have kids we can add on to the cottage and have a beautiful lakefront home."

Erica does not realize that her relationship with Frank helps subsidize his marriage, and that his words of love and plans for the future are only fantasies.

About two years into their affair, Erica started asking Frank when he was leaving Gloria. He changed the subject or made a joke. But he became more and more nervous about Erica's expectations. He didn't want to disappoint her but he was not about to have Gloria find out about the affair. He started imagining what a disaster it could become and how angry Gloria would be. When Frank ended his affair, he missed Erica and worried about her. He called her every week to be sure she was OK.

Frank now says, "Overall the affair with Erica was great. It helped me through a rough time in my marriage. Erica is a great gal and we had fun. I feel a little guilty that she was so upset."

Erica was astonished when Frank said he couldn't see her anymore. She exclaimed, "I could not believe what he was saying. What about our love and our plans? Frank said he just couldn't leave his kids."

Six months after the end of the affair Erica still thought Frank might come back. She says, "I know how much he loves me and how hard this is for him. He still calls and we talk. His marriage isn't any better and I respect him for trying to make it work."

Both men and women feel hurt and sorrow when their affair ends, especially if it is their first affair. Men and women feel very differently about subsequent affairs. Women feel about the same amount of pain from one affair to the next—men don't. When men decide to have another affair, they are more careful about how involved they become and how dependent on them they allow their lover to be.

Reasons Men Have Pain During Affairs
(in order of importance)

1. Guilt in relation to spouse
2. Fear of being found out
3. Deceit
4. Hurt to the marriage
5. Guilt in relation to children
6. Other's jealousy
7. Own jealous feelings

—Lawson

A couple of years after Frank's affair with Erica he had an affair with a co-worker, Joan. This time Frank was more careful about making it clear that he only wanted an affair and would not get a divorce. He recounts, "I learned one thing from the affair with Erica—you have to protect yourself from their really falling for you. It was a year or so after I broke up with Erica before she dated again. I felt bad about that. This time I told Joan, 'We will have fun, enjoy sex and be friends, but no strings. I will not leave my wife.' I'm also more cautious about complaining to her about Gloria. In fact, I don't talk about my wife at all."

Joan's first affair had been with a former college boyfriend, Denny. As she describes it, "I fell hard for Denny. I thought I was in love and I thought he loved me. I think I got too possessive and demanding. I just didn't give him enough space, and our affair ended.

"This time I am more rational about love. I decided to have an affair with Frank because my marriage is dead and I need someone to be close to. I would get a divorce, but financially I cannot afford to. Frank is a great guy. He is the kind of guy I should have married. He is successful, well respected, caring

CHART 32   **Degree of Unhappiness Men Feel from Affairs**
Lawson, 1988

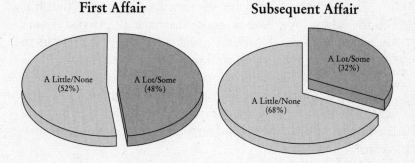

First Affair

A Little/None
(52%)

A Lot/Some
(48%)

Subsequent Affair

A Lot/Some
(32%)

A Little/None
(68%)

and sensitive. He has made it clear that he doesn't plan on a divorce, but I guess most people don't."

Frank believes he has made it clear to Joan that he is committed to his marriage; still she has hope. Frank is a desirable husband and he could solve her financial problems. In the meantime, Joan doesn't try to solve her marriage or her financial issues because she is irrationallly counting on Frank.

Joan admits, "I'll be pretty devastated if this affair ends. Part of me knows it will, but I cannot stop myself from loving Frank. I am very conscious of not becoming too clingy because I know that would drive him away. I know he has a lot of feeling for me. That is obvious in the way he treats me."

Like Joan, very few women can separate sex from emotional involvement, so whether it is their first or third affair they feel just as much pain and disappointment when it ends. Sometimes more, because they see the end of the affair as another failure to find love. One thing that is different for women after their first affair is that they think they will be able to protect themselves better and keep their expectations in check. However, that seldom turns out to be true.

Frank is thoughtful and loving and he does treat Joan well, but for Frank, his relationship with Joan is only an affair.

Frank's wife, Gloria, has no idea about Frank's other life. Gloria says, "We have a good marriage. I married Frank because he is an all-around good guy. He is successful in everything he does. He is well respected professionally. He is a great dad; the kids adore him. He contributes generously to charities and he has lots of friends. As a husband, I couldn't ask for more. He is supportive, considerate, loving and respectful. I love him dearly. What more could a woman want?"

Frank and Gloria believe they have a good marriage. Frank's affairs do not indicate that he is unhappy in his marriage.

▼ "SUCCESSFUL" MEN DO NOT MARRY THEIR LOVERS

Successful men (executives, entrepreneurs, professionals and salesmen) are sexual outside marriage, but they rarely divorce their wife, then marry their lover, according to a study by Jan Halper, Ph.D.

In *Quiet Desperation*, Dr. Halper writes, "Nearly eighty percent of the men who had affairs told me the reason they stay in their marriage is because they are afraid no one else would tolerate them the way their wife does. They are dependent on her. They appreciate her because of all the inconsideration she puts up with. They have fun with their lovers, but it is their wives who stick by them and whom they fall back on for security. When an affair satisfies their needs, they return to their marriage a happier person. Unfortunately for the lovers, the benefits of their love, effort and hard work are reaped by the wife." *Only 3% of the 4,100 successful men surveyed eventually married their lover.*

CHART 33   **Percentage of "Successful" Men Who Marry Their Extramarital Lover**

Halper, 1988

Even when "successful" men divorce, they rarely marry the woman with whom they had an affair.

▼ "SUCCESSFUL" AFFAIRS

Lovers consider their affair successful when it enhances their lives. When lovers are able to meet needs without sacrificing the quality of life they have created for themselves and their families, they consider their affair to be a positive experience. Affairs that are undiscovered, especially if they occur in the workplace without the knowledge of co-workers, are also regarded as positive experiences.

Expectations play a major role in how lovers experience the affair. Affairees who see the affair as a minor part of their life feel good about their affair and themselves.

Those who expect the relationship to become a marriage or the center of their lives are often bitter and nearly always disappointed. Men and women may choose an affair to meet needs that have not been met in their marriage. This does not mean they intend to replace their spouse with their lover, even when they express such a wish.

Most affairees make conscious choices to limit the level of their involvement and are protective of their marriage and family. When their needs are met they go back to their family, feeling enriched.

When both lovers share the expectation that the affair will be a short-term intense and pleasurable relationship that enhances their lives, they have positive feelings about their experience, but it is not without other consequences. Both men and women experience emotional pain—and sometimes affairs have unexpected life-altering consequences.

▶ 9

Ending the Affair

Affairs are easier to begin than to end.

Love affairs are hard to quit. Lovers miss one another for a long time—months and years, not days and weeks. They often wonder if they made the right decision. The end of an affair brings with it a grieving process that lasts about a year. Feelings of anger, hurt, loneliness and even depression will linger. The affairee will feel betrayed, lonely and deceived (even if there were no promises). Everyone involved feels pain for a time, and all will grieve the loss of what was and what could have been.

Love affairs don't just evaporate, nor do they end with celebration. If you decide to end your love affair, talk to your lover, don't just stop showing up or start making excuses. Negligence breeds rage and a desire for retaliation. It is better to face the anger, hurt and disappointment than to have it surface in some other way.

Bert recalls, "When Lillian and I started our affair we were very clear with one another that it would not interfere with our marriages. We were both committed to our families.

"I don't think either of us expected to fall in love but we did. We had been lovers for about two years when Lillian started making excuses about getting together. The more she pulled away the more I wanted her.

"She said she still loved me but had to work, or take care of her kids, or do something with her husband. I guess I should have seen the handwriting on the wall but I didn't. I felt desperate and I wanted to be with her.

"I let my wife know I wasn't happy and I wasn't in love with her anymore. She was devastated. I called Lillian three or four times every day—at work, at home, on her cellular.

"One afternoon last spring Lillian angrily told me to leave her alone. She didn't want to see me anymore, she didn't want me to call her. She wanted me out of her life. She reminded me that this was just a fling and we had agreed not to let it interfere with our lives. She was mad!

"I alternated between feeling like a fool and thinking of telling her husband. I guess I wanted her life to be as much of a mess as mine."

Lillian's refusal to tell Bert the truth when she wanted to end the affair only made things worse. As difficult as it would have been to see him hurt, not telling him made him feel more desperate and vindictive.

The end of an affair has the same stages of grief as the death of a person.

Stages of Grief

1. Denial and Isolation—disbelief, rejection and alienation
2. Anger—rage, envy, hatred and resentment
3. Bargaining—prayers and promises, negotiation and compromise

4. Depression—numbness, loss and loneliness
5. Acceptance—knowing, understanding and believing
   Elizabeth Kübler-Ross

▼ BREAKING UP IS HARD TO DO

Tell your lover your decision without excuses. Trying to discuss all the "whys" only provokes unwanted negotiation and pain. The simple truth is best. Ending the affair does not mean ending your feelings. You will miss one another and continue to feel the desire to be together. When you are thinking about your lover, remind yourself of the hassles and hurts. Dwell on the problems, not the romance or the sex.

Reduce the opportunities to see your lover. Schedule time with your family or friends at the times you have been seeing your lover. Commit time and energy to creating new experiences for yourself and your spouse. Seek counseling if you need someone to talk to in order to meet the emotional void you feel. Be sure the counselor knows that your goal is to end the affair.

Adam frowns as he recalls, "I think I did a good job ending my affair with Rachel. I told her I loved her as my friend but I was committed to my marriage and going on longer would just be worse.

"At first she just cried, then didn't want to see me at all. I called every other day just to see how she was doing. After a week she agreed to see me.

"We talked about how to end our affair just as we had talked when we started. One of the great things about our relationship was how well we communicated.

"We decided we would talk twice a week and see each other once a week in a public place during the day—nothing romantic. We talked about our lives and what we were doing to get through this. We gave each other suggestions on coping with our loss.

"After about three months we only talked on the phone about once a week. Now we haven't talked for about six months. I still think about her and I miss her but I feel good about the affair from beginning to end."

▼ ━━━━━━━━━━━━━━━━━━━━━━━━━━━

How to End the Affair

1. Tell your lover you are ending the affair.

2. Remind yourself of the hassles and problems of the affair; don't fantasize about sex or romance.

3. Remember, lying leaves you feeling bad about yourself.

4. Schedule time with family or friends when you usually see your lover.

5. Be accountable to your spouse for your time and whereabouts.

6. Become more involved with your spouse.

7. Plan new experiences for yourself.

8. Find a counselor.

9. Expect to feel sad, hurt and lonely at times.

10. Remember, your feelings will change.

━━━━━━━━━━━━━━━━━━━━━━━━━━━

▶ 10

Changing Course: Leaving Your Marriage to Be with Your Lover

▼ Unexpected Problems

Many of the risks of an affair have already been identified. Several others have surfaced during my counseling experience. While *Fatal Attraction* is just a movie, life can be even stranger than fiction. Both men and women can become obsessed or malicious, with or without provocation. While lovers seldom directly tell the affairee's spouse of the affair, the lover may decide to inform the affairee's employer, colleagues, parents or children.

One obvious risk men often overlook in their affairs is pregnancy. Do not assume the woman will take care of birth control. A woman may secretly plan to have a baby, or she may decide to keep a baby even if the pregnancy was not planned. Men should remember that if a woman is pregnant, she may believe it is entirely her decision about giving birth, and *his* lifetime responsibility. People often do not act as planned, and the unexpected can change your life.

These are a few of the unexpected problems my clients have encountered:

▸ James's affair lasted less than two months. His affairee's sister sent a copy of a sexually explicit love letter to his wife. The letter also stated that he had never loved his wife and that he had had many other affairs. The letter was a fake.

▸ Clara's lover contacted her parents and told them of the affair. He went into detail about how she had seduced him and tried to break up his marriage. Her parents were distraught and frightened.

▸ Jeremy only had sex with his affairee twice and regretted it immediately. She had not told him she had herpes. He passed on the herpes virus to his wife while she was pregnant.

▸ Kitty never actually had sex with her affairee but nonetheless he became infatuated and obsessed with her. He followed her everywhere—in the mornings to work and returning home at night, he was always there. She spoke with the police. They could do nothing because there was no crime. She was terrified for her children, her husband and herself. She didn't know what he might do.

▸ Andrew's lover became pregnant, although she had told him she was on the pill. She had the baby and agreed to confidentiality in exchange for a one-time payment of $75,000. He paid the money. A year later she filed a paternity suit.

Not one of these people ever anticipated the nightmare that followed their affair. After all, no one knowingly chooses a lover who would be deliberately destructive, but bad things do happen.

▼ DECIDING TO LEAVE YOUR MARRIAGE TO BE WITH YOUR LOVER

The passion, the desire and the intensity you feel when you "fall in love" seem strong enough to last. Dreams are interwoven, promises are made and a married life may be built on this foundation.

Then the feelings change, the dreams fade and the promises are broken. Not only do the feelings for the spouse change, but many begin to feel those same wonderful, intense feelings for someone new. We want to be "in love" with the person we marry. We believe in love and in marriage, but the notion of a romantic love that lasts a lifetime is unrealistic. A marriage based only on feelings does not stand a very good chance of long-term survival.

Fewer than 10% of affairs result in marriage between the affairees. The same issues that were problematic in first marriages occur in subsequent marriages, along with a host of new ones.

Affairs are easy relationships because of their limitations. Gil found his affair so much easier and more rewarding than his marriage that he decided on a divorce. Gil recounts, "My marriage paled by comparison. Jeannie and I seemed to think alike; it hurt to be apart. I divorced Helen. Jeannie knew we would have less money but didn't care. Well, that was two years ago. Now money seems to be all we talk about. Every time I want to give my son a little extra money, she has a fit. Now she wants a child of her own, a bigger house and she doesn't want to work full-time.

"Jeannie's complaints are the same as Helen's: I don't listen to her and I won't talk to her. She is right, I don't want to talk to her. I have heard what she has to say. I can never seem to make her happy. I would like to have fun, too. What about sex? That was fun.

"This relationship is impossible. Being married to Helen was easy by comparison. We didn't always agree but life was simpler. I thought our disagreements meant we weren't happy."

Gil ended his first marriage not understanding that marriage is a very difficult relationship. He thought he had chosen the wrong woman and if he just married the right one everything would be fine. It wasn't. Gil and Jeannie started their divorce a year after their marriage.

▼ REMARRIAGE

Subsequent marriage, or remarriage, is most successful when there are few differences between the new spouses. Most successful remarriages are between people with similar socioeconomic backgrounds, education levels and ages.

Remarriages do not turn out to be happier than first marriages. In fact, there is very little difference in the degree of happiness or unhappiness from one marriage to the next. However, remarriages are much less stable than first marriages. Ex-wives and ex-husbands who know the affair occurred prior to their divorce carry a lifetime of resentment and hostility toward the new spouse, making the new marriage even more difficult.

While affairees may believe their love will conquer all of life's challenges, the duration of affair-remarriages is short and the long-term divorce rate is over 75%.

Adrian hated conflict and he had always been a peacemaker. When he started his affair with Becca everything was so easy. No conflict or anger. They didn't argue about anything. He and his wife, Melanie, seemed to argue all the time. Adrian could hardly wait to marry Becca.

In less than a year Adrian divorced Melanie, leaving her with three young children. Adrian ran his own business and made plenty of money so he thought he could take care of two families and everyone would be fine. He had it all figured out in his mind. He would let Melanie and the kids stay in the house and he would continue to pay all their expenses. Becca had a good income and he could pull more money out of the business for them to live on. He had been away from home so much anyway he figured he would actually see the kids more and have quality time with them every other weekend and Wednesdays.

Becca thought having part-time kids would be perfect. She told her friends, "Adrian's kids are darling. They are fun to play with, cute and well-behaved. We will be great part-time parents together. We will have the joy of children and still have plenty of time for each other."

Of course, nothing turns out as planned. Melanie was outraged and devastated. She fell into a major depression and had difficulty caring for her children. Both Adrian's parents and Melanie's parents were furious with him.

Adrian was confused. He complained, "When I offer to take the kids more and go home to help Melanie out with the house, then Becca is mad. My youngest son, age 4, started wetting the bed at night, my older son has night terrors. My daughter is great. She behaves like a little angel. She wants to help Daddy. I think she is the only one who cares about me."

Between taking care of his children and working later at night to earn extra money to support two households, Adrian found that his new marriage began to feel the pressure. He reminded Becca, "You wanted to parent my kids. Now if I ask you to take one of them to a ball game or go pick them up you make a big deal of it. I can't be everything to everybody."

CHART 34
National Center Health Statistics, 1983

Men & Women	Duration of Remarriage
Once Divorced	10.8 Years
Twice Divorced	7 Years
Thrice Divorced	5 Years

Becca exploded, "You certainly aren't everything to me. Between your kids, your work and always trying to prove you are a good guy there isn't much left for me."

Becca and Adrian stayed together for four years, then she moved out. She told Adrian, "This is not what I signed up for. I wanted marriage, romance and a buddy. I get none of these things from you. You won't deal with anything. We have problems and you won't talk. You withdraw and sulk. I'm sick of you moping around feeling sorry for yourself. I'm finished."

Adrian looked at her without expression. He just said, "OK." He didn't know what else he could have done. In counseling he explained tearfully, "I tried to take care of everybody. I did the best I could. I'm exhausted. I thought Becca would love my kids. She just created tension with Melanie and she was always criticizing the boys and telling me how to treat my daughter. All this and I end up divorced again—unbelievable."

Remarriage is twice as complicated as first marriages if there are children. Just the number of people involved creates chaos for most families. Everyone needs resources: time, energy and money. There doesn't ever seem to be enough. A stepparent does not have the same relationship a biological parent has with a child. These stepparent and biological parent relationships are nearly always a source of trouble.

▼ REASONS AFFAIR-REMARRIAGES FAIL

Frank Pittman, psychiatrist and author of *Private Lies,* interviewed 100 of his patients to identify the role of affairs in marriage, divorce and remarriage. He found the divorce rate among those who married their lovers to be 75%. My experience is consistent with his: of twenty-one affair-remarriages, only four couples remain married fifteen years later. Dr. Pittman's patients identified the following reasons their affair-remarriage did not last:

- ▸ Intervention of reality
- ▸ Guilt
- ▸ Disparity of sacrifice
- ▸ Expectations
- ▸ General distrust of marriage
- ▸ Distrust of affairee
- ▸ Divided loyalty
- ▸ Nature of affairees
- ▸ Romance
- ▸ Scapegoating
- ▸ Lack of shared histories

In addition to having to share resources with a former family, affair-remarriage partners have a lot of emotional baggage. Trust is hard to create. Each spouse knows the other can lie

CHART 35   **Percentage of Divorces Among Affairees
Who Marry Their Lover**

Pittman, 1989

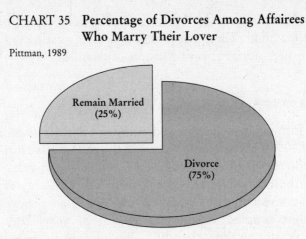

*Affairees who marry one another have a very high divorce rate. Fewer
than half who remain married are happy.*

and cheat, even though they tell themselves that it was different then. It is hard for people to believe their marriage will not
and cannot be like their affair.

▶ 11

Facts on Divorce

"A 1989 study of U.S. Census records shows a divorce rate
for first marriages at 67%. Second marriages do worse!"
    —JOHN GOTTMAN, *WHY MARRIAGES SUCCEED
    OR FAIL*, 1994

One of the most in-depth, long-term studies on divorce is
Second Chances by Judith Wallerstein and Sandra Blakeslee.
They interviewed and assessed sixty families in the process of
divorce. Ten years later they contacted these families and studied the consequences and benefits of their divorces. They
noted that while *a few people* found greater happiness with a
new spouse, there were many second and even third divorces,
and the children had lifetime disadvantages.

Henry shakes his head sadly as he tells his story: "I didn't
really know what marriage was. I thought the euphoria I felt
before we were married would last. Evelyn was all I could
think about and I had no interest in looking at any other
woman. I really loved her when we got married.

"By our second anniversary I felt something was missing,
but we decided to have a baby. I thought that would help.

"The baby just made things worse. I found more things about Evelyn I didn't like, and she didn't seem all that enamored with me either. She was always complaining she was tired and needed more from me. I wanted her to get more organized.

"We were always bickering. Mostly a lot of little things. She wanted to go out more, you know, the things women like to do—dancing, dinners, romantic movies—but I was determined not to be henpecked. I wasn't going to miss a football or baseball game for some silly romantic thing.

"She wanted to go to counseling but I said, 'You can't change a leopard's spots. No stranger is going to tell me what to do. I like myself the way I am.'

"By our fourth anniversary we had separate lives. I started seeing other women, and she went out with her girlfriends. Our sex life was nearly nonexistent. Later that year we separated. I missed our daughter but I thought I would be a better parent if I was happy."

Henry lacked an understanding of how marriage works. He had no sense of what it takes to make a marriage a partnership. He thought feelings would be enough. Rather than trying to understand what Evelyn wanted, he became more determined to have his way and prove he was in control.

After his divorce, Henry had six failed relationships before he came to counseling. Initially he complained, "I just don't understand women." As he came to understand how his concern about control alienated him from the people he cared about, he made choices that took into account the wishes of his dates as well as his own. As he became more confident about his ability to communicate and negotiate, he was able to relax his need for control. He came to genuinely enjoy women. He began to see that a woman could offer ideas and new experiences that added to his life rather than take something from him.

Henry continues, "Both Evelyn and I remarried. In retrospect what Evelyn wanted was no different than what other women expected. It was no big deal. Now I make an effort to please my wife, to find out what she would like and do it with her. I aim to please her rather than resist. I like doing things with her—going to plays, concerts, movies, dinner—and I like talking to her and learning to be a better husband and lover. If I would have done the same things with Evelyn I think we would have been happy and our daughter would have grown up with both parents."

Marriage takes skill, determination and insight. Many people find out during their second or third marriage that the same problems recur over and over. In time most realize that unless they change, one marriage is not much better than the other. In fact, subsequent marriages are harder and often end in another divorce.

Before you opt for a divorce, thinking a new marriage will be better or easier, try learning new skills and becoming a more giving and flexible partner in your current marriage. Divorce doesn't usually make anyone happier for long.

▼ MEN AND DIVORCE

Divorce is easier for men—initially. Men find both dating and remarriage easier than women do, but their long-term prospects in another marriage hold risks.

Men who marry the woman with whom they have an affair generally live with the animosity of their former wife and children. One-half of divorced women and one-third of divorced men are intensely angry a decade after their divorce.

Men remarry sooner and more often than women of the same age, but their chances of another failed marriage are high, especially with a substantially younger wife. The second divorce is usually initiated by the wife. Of those 25% who remain remarried, fewer than half are happy in their new marriage.

Myron wanted a divorce. He had not ever been very happy in his marriage. He and his wife, Salina, had two kids within two years after they were married. He remembers, "I felt like an outsider much of the time. It seemed like all Salina's energy went into the kids. As the saying goes, we grew apart. She had her life and I had mine.

"I started seeing Bonnie about six months before our divorce. She really didn't have anything to do with it. She sort of gave us an excuse to do something about our empty marriage. I saw Bonnie for about a year after our divorce but she wasn't the right woman either. I dated a bunch of women after Bonnie—no one special. I spent time with my kids, Wednesdays and every other weekend, and that was a hassle for some of the women I dated. They wanted to do one thing, the kids another. It just didn't work out.

"Two years later I met June. She had everything. She was fifteen years younger than I, beautiful, smart, fun and exciting. She could even manage my kids. When I had them she would plan a movie, make a great dinner or figure out something for them to do. We got married and everything changed almost immediately. She started making more demands. She wanted more of my time. She wanted to go out more, she wanted to make more rules for my kids, she wanted to talk more, on and on. Five years later she wants a divorce. Boy, did she change. She is certainly not the girl I married."

Myron believes in someone who doesn't exist. He looks for a perfect woman who will make the relationship work around him. He sees the needs other people have as a problem or a burden—even those of his children. He believes someone else will make him happy. Unfortunately, for men like Myron, in over twenty years of counseling I have never seen it work out.

CHART 36

10 Years after divorce	Dangers	Opportunities
Men	33% Intensely angry after a decade	Freedom from stress
	50% Get divorced again	50% Happily remarried
	80% Same/lower quality of life	20% Better quality of life
	See kids emotionally damaged	Personal growth
	Conflict or alienation with kids	Better relations with kids
Under 50 years old	50% Unhappily remarried	50% Happily remarried
Over 50 years old	66% Unhappily remarried	33% Happily remarried

▼ WOMEN AND DIVORCE

Women feel good about a divorce only if they initiated it. They also usually find themselves with a lower standard of living and most of the responsibility for child-rearing. Occasionally, women give up custody of their children (less than 10%). The likelihood of a woman remarrying is directly related to her age. The younger the woman, the greater her chance of remarriage. While women report that the second marriage is not more satisfying than the first, they are likely to avoid a second divorce by lowering their expectations, becoming more flexible and more giving.

Karen was 30 when she and Barry divorced. "Our divorce was amicable," she admits. "Partly because I thought starting over in a new marriage would not be that hard. I was wrong. I dated maybe twenty men before I met Ed. Some were world-class jerks.

"Ed is a great guy and we had a good time together and he liked my kids. I had been married to Ed for about two years when he said, 'I don't think I can do this kid thing again.' I was afraid this was coming; I knew he didn't like the way I dealt with the kids. He thought they were spoiled. He went on to say, 'Look, I raised my kids and I thought I could help you with yours, but all we do is argue about them. They are ruining our marriage. Couldn't their dad take them during the week and we could have them three days a week? That is about as much time as we spend with them anyway.'

"As much as I knew it wasn't the same seeing them weekends and once during the week, I also knew their father could take good care of them and that my marriage would not survive their teenage years.

"I asked their dad if we could try reversing the custody arrangement. He was eager to have them. Having two teenagers was hard on their dad's wife and I guess they ended up going to marriage counseling.

"It has worked out pretty well. They have both graduated from college now and they are healthy, happy, well-adjusted adults. Ed and I have a good relationship with each other and I have a close relationship with my kids. They aren't too fond of Ed but they are polite. I think it probably worked out best for everyone, although it hurt to let them go. I cried myself to sleep many nights."

Divorce is hard and remarriage is even harder. As delightful as children can be, they usually add stress and discord to a new marriage. Women rarely give up custody of their children, but if they do it is usually to save their marriage.

Worldwide, women over 40 who can financially afford to live independently do not remarry by their choice. Unfortunately, few women are in this situation, and most never financially recover from a divorce.

CHART 37

10 Years After Divorce	Dangers	Opportunities
Women	50% remain angry a decade after divorce	Stops conflict and violence
	73% lower living standard	Ends bad marriage
		Better self-esteem
	Find life as a single parent difficult	Better self-confidence
	See their kids with emotional problems	80% glad they initiated divorce
20-30 years old	52% single	48% remarry
30-40 years old	66% single	33% remarry
40-50 years old	89% single	11% remarry
50 years or older	97% single	3% remarry

▼ CHILDREN AND DIVORCE

There is no correlation between how children react to divorce initially and the amount of damage found ten years later. Children often suffer long-term damage from the reduction of their parents' resources: time, energy and money.

Divorced parents spend less time with children, provide fewer educational opportunities and often look to the children for emotional support rather than providing it. Children from divorced families are less likely to complete college, often because fathers and mothers are unable or unwilling to pay for their tuition and support.

Wallerstein and Blakeslee found that "Only one child in eight saw both parents recover from divorce in happy remarriage." The only children who seemed to benefit from divorce, according to their study, were those whose home life involved continual conflict or abuse.

Ellis says, "I was twelve and my brother, Scott, was eight when my parents split up. I knew it was coming. Just the way they talked to each other, and Dad was gone so much. I had lots of friends whose dads didn't live with them so I wasn't afraid but it was hard. Mom was always so stressed out.

"Dad was a great guy and came for us every week. It always seemed like Mom was bitching at him. They argued just like they had before they got divorced.

"Dad got remarried to a nice woman named Ruth. She had two kids, too. She was nice to me and I liked her but it wasn't like being home. Weekends were a hassle. I felt like I was in their way, and I couldn't play with my friends.

"After Dad got married, Mom seemed to be more angry and money was all she talked about. If I needed money for school or camp, she always said, 'Ask your dad—he's the one with the money.' I hated hearing that 'he's the one' over and over, so I quit asking.

"When I graduated from college, Mom and Dad both came but Mom wouldn't sit with Dad and Ruth. It was hard to always have to choose between them.

"I got angry with Mom for always criticizing Dad. He did the best he could. It made me want to get away from her and away from home.

"My brother, Scott, dropped out of college. By then everybody was complaining about money—Dad, Ruth and Mom. Ruth said her former husband wasn't giving her enough. Mom said Dad didn't give her enough. Dad said he just didn't have any more. He and Ruth needed a bigger house, Ruth needed a new car, her kids needed orthodontia. Scott quit asking for anything and went to work. He thought he could work and go to school but he couldn't. Now he works in a hardware store and hangs out. He's pretty lonely and I think he drinks a lot."

Ellis and Scott's experience is a familiar one. Divorced fam-

CHART 38
Wallerstein, 1989

10 Years After Divorce	Dangers	Opportunities
Kids	88% parents remain angry	Relief of stress
	40% boys without college or career focus	Learn from mistakes of parents
	88% see at least one parent suffer long-term emotional damage	See better remarriage
	50% quit college	
	+50% see second divorce	
	50% are less successful in college and work than counterpart in intact families	
	50% kids angry, many boys violent	
	Lower self esteem	

ilies simply do not have the same resources for their children that intact families have. Money is often singled out as the main reason boys drop out of college, but it is also probably a lack of guidance and determination from their fathers. Most fathers remarry, and their emotional and physical energy cannot be fully devoted to their sons.

▼ DIVORCE LONG-TERM

The impact of divorce lasts a lifetime for everyone involved. Many, perhaps most, never fully recover from its effects. Even short-term, divorce is a long process. It takes between two and three years to develop a stable post-divorce life.

Divorce does present some opportunities, but with significant costs to all. In only 10% of divorces does everyone end up with an equally good quality of life.

CHART 39
Wallerstein, 1989

	Women	Men
After Divorce Years to Recovery	3.0–3.5	2.5–3.0

CHART 40 Quality of Life Ten Years after Divorce
Wallerstein, 1989

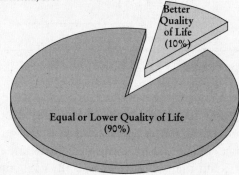

Only about 10% of couples who divorce can create a better quality of life for themselves.

▼ FROM A DISTANCE—MARRIAGE LOOKS BETTER

Five to ten years after divorce, most men have remarried. Many have second families. But they are not without regrets. It turns out the spouse may not have been the problem after all. A survey for *Cosmopolitan* magazine showed that nearly 80% of the men said they would remarry their former wife

given the chance. Economic problems that arise from supporting two families contribute to conflict, hurt, guilt and resentment between children and parents and new spouses. *The
needs that were once overwhelming vanish—making this marriage no better than the former marriage.*

While this survey was not scientific, it gives us a glimpse of
what men think and feel about their divorce years later. I do
not find this percentage surprising, as many of the men I have
interviewed made the same comments.

Abbott says, "I was determined to get a divorce. Our marriage was not working. She complained constantly, gained
twenty pounds and went shopping every day. I hated my life
and I blamed Julie for changing and getting fat. We had no sex.
At that time I considered these to be impossible problems.

CHART 41   **Percentage of Men Who Say They Would
             Remarry Former Wife**

Cosmopolitan, Sept. 1992

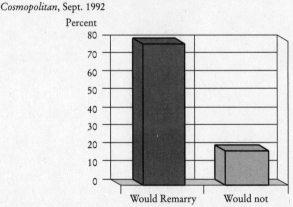

Given the chance, nearly 80% of the men surveyed said they would remarry their ex-wife.

"Eight years after our divorce Julie looks great. She lost probably twenty-five pounds, exercises every day and loves her job. She is a good mother and her new husband seems to be happy. The bad part of the divorce is the kids. I try not to think about it too much, 'cause I don't like some other guy raising my kids. I can't give the kids what I could have if we had stayed together. If we could go back would I remarry Julie? You bet!"

► 12

Refocusing on Your Marriage

▼ REFOCUSING ON YOUR MARRIAGE

Marriage is one of our biggest investments. It requires continuous maintenance.

The discovery of an affair stresses the emotional fiber of a marriage, resulting in a chaotic and confusing array of feelings for both spouses. There is an intrinsic need to distance from the spouse emotionally, perhaps from guilt, uncertainty or internal conflict. The affairee often becomes critical or angry with the spouse. The small tensions that were formerly over-looked, or were even endearing, become a focal point for criticism, dislike or condemnation.

Even when a spouse is not consciously aware of an affair, they may have an intuitive sense of it. It is common for spouses to realize, once an affair is confessed, that they had feelings or doubts they tried to ignore. The spouse may feel afraid, and because they do not know the basis of their fear, the feeling is expressed as criticism. While it is possible to feel love for more than one person at a time, we are seldom able to be "in love" with two people simultaneously—at least not for very long.

The spouse who feels betrayed will have feelings that range from fear to sorrow to rage. The spouse will grieve the loss of trust they once took for granted; both spouse and affairee will grieve the loss of their innocence.

There is considerable controversy about whether to confess your affair to your spouse. In making your decision, be clear about your motivation. If it is simply to make yourself feel better, don't do it. If you want to reinvest in your marriage, confession can be helpful.

Before you decide, read the following two sections and be sure that if you confess you are willing to commit the time, energy and skills necessary to promote your spouse's eventual well-being over the course of many years.

▼ SPOUSE'S KNOWLEDGE OF AFFAIR

About half of spouses know about their partner's first love affair. The spouse's knowledge of an affair depends to a large

CHART 42 | **Percentage of Spouses Who Know of the Affair**
Spanier & Margolis, 1983

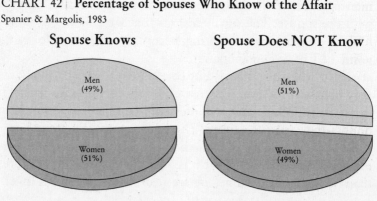

degree on the type of affair, its intensity and its duration. When people are "in love," it shows. Attitudes, behavior and appearance all reflect the feelings and choices of the lovers. Loving affairs are often suspected but not usually discovered. Sex affairs are seldom revealed, except when health problems occur.

When an affair is confessed, it is usually the first one; subsequent affairs are more carefully concealed.

▼ CONFESSION

While affairees often believe their affair has only minor effects on their marriage, they believe confessing has more impact, especially for women. The majority of women report that confessing their affair had a negative impact on their marriages. Negative impacts include the spouse's hurt or anger, emotional alienation and loss of trust.

A small portion of men and women—20%—claim that confessing their affair had a "positive impact" on their marriage. These positive impacts include greater attentiveness to one another, renewal of emotional bonds and more sex.

Rarely does the admission of an affair cause divorce, if the marriage is otherwise healthy and happy.

Amber's eyes well up as she tells of Randall's confession: "When Randall said, 'We need to talk,' I knew what he was going to tell me, ironically. I hadn't thought he was having an affair, but suddenly I knew he was. It was a strange feeling.

"He started by assuring me he loved me and wanted to be married to me. Then in a trembling voice he said, 'I saw someone—a girl from work. I'm ashamed, it was a terrible mistake, and I have no excuse. I just want to put this behind us and make it up to you.'

"Part of me felt like laughing but I was crying. We both

cried. He said, 'I will tell you everything or nothing—whatever is best for you. I don't want to lose you or the love we have. I think we should go to counseling and find out the best way to get ourselves through this.' As horrible as his confession was, I felt oddly safe and secure with Randall. I could see from the agony he was feeling how sorry he was, but beyond that was his concern for me. He kept coming back to me and how I felt and what I needed.

"A friend had told me about her husband's confession after his affair. He had a thousand excuses. He blamed his wife for not being home more. He blamed his lover for seducing him. Even then what he wanted was for his wife to 'forgive' him. He wasn't offering anything. Somehow everything was *her* fault and she should simply forgive him and forget it as though nothing had happened. I thought at the time, if Randall ever did that I would divorce him on the spot.

"But that wasn't how Randall treated me. I know he did the same thing, but I felt more loved, cared about and valued. Anyone can make mistake. It is how you handle it that matters. Am I angry? Sometimes, but not like I would have imagined. Hurt? Yes, but again it was not so bad. Love and respect? Yes, more than ever. I probably am more careful with our marriage now, more tuned-in, but I wouldn't say suspicious. In fact, I trust Randall maybe more than before because I see how much I mean to him."

Randall's confession was successful and helped to rebuild a stronger marriage. Taylor had the opposite experience when she confessed.

Taylor looks distraught as she reflects, "I told Isaac because I thought it would clear the slate and we could start over. I thought being honest would help, he would forgive me, and I wouldn't have to feel guilty. I was way wrong. He was annihilated. He couldn't sleep, he cried out at night, he lost twelve pounds. It was hell watching him suffer for what I had done. Confessing didn't end up making me less guilty and it did not help our marriage at all. It has been a year and I don't know if he can ever get past this. Confessing only hurt, it didn't heal anybody."

Taylor believes confessing her affair did far more damage than good. Isaac did get past the shock and betrayal he felt, but both agree she should have dealt with the problem herself. Their marriage survived her affair, but confessing certainly didn't make it better.

Kevin also decided to confess his affair. He had good intentions. Kevin told Loretta about his affair six months after it was over. He had learned from his affair how to be more intimate and to communicate his feelings better. He thought if he told Loretta how much he loved her and wanted to be closer and more intimate, she would forgive him.

When he confessed he told her how deeply he regretted his choice and how selfish he had been. He said he had learned how much she meant to him and how important their marriage was. He assured her he would do whatever it took to make it up to her.

Loretta was enraged. She screamed, "Get out. I never want to see you again." Kevin didn't leave. He tried to hold her but she wouldn't let him touch her. She said, "I told you if this ever happened we were through—and we are. I want a divorce." Over the next six months Kevin tried to persuade Loretta of his love and regret but she was steadfast. She wouldn't let him touch her even affectionately, let alone sexually. She refused to talk to him about anything other than the business of living. He kept hoping she would soften but she didn't.

A year and a half later he started another affair. He says, "It is just a matter of time until I give Loretta the divorce she wants. Now she says she doesn't want a divorce but she'll never trust me again. She says she doesn't think she can ever be intimate with me again. I regret I had the affair. I was being stupid. But I am really sorry I ever told Loretta. Maybe we wouldn't have ever been very close but I wouldn't be permanently in the doghouse."

Kevin's conclusion is only partly true. His confession made the relationship worse, but the real mistake was the affair. Kevin and Loretta had problems confiding their feelings to one another before the affair. Rather than confront his disappointment then, Kevin simply went elsewhere to get those needs met. Kevin and Loretta were not able to bridge the emotional gap between them before the affair. Once Loretta's trust in him was shattered, she was unable to meet him halfway to rebuild the marriage.

While most marriages have enough resilience to survive an affair, some don't and the amount of emotional damage is beyond repair.

CHART 43 Affairees Report of the Impact Confessing Their Affair Had on Their Marriage

Lawson, 1988

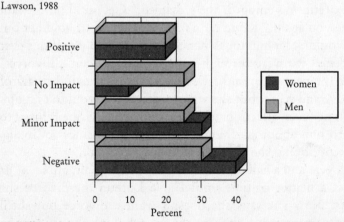

Most affairees believe confessing their affair had an impact on their marriage. The impact is more negative for women who confess.

If you decide to confess, keep the focus on your spouse. Expect that they will be hurt, angry and frightened. Do not get defensive.

How to Confess

- Choose a time when you are both able to talk without interruption.
- Reassure your spouse about your love and commitment.
- Keep the truth simple and accept the responsibility for your choices.
- Talk about yourself and your feelings, not about your lover or your spouse.
- Be redundantly clear with your spouse in stating that you want to restore your marriage.
- Listen patiently, like a friend, to your spouse's feelings and thoughts.
- Keep focused on your spouse's feelings, fears, outrage and pain.

When Confessing...

- *Do not* use alcohol or drugs.
- *Do not* blame or criticize your spouse.
- *Do not* blame your lover.
- *Do not* lie.
- *Do not* tell all the gory details; they hurt.
- *Do not* frighten or threaten your spouse.
- *Do not* defend or justify your actions.
- *Do not* leave!

▼ SUMMARY

An affair is not the end of your marriage—unless you want it to be.

An affair is just an affair. It is a slice of life. It feels better than any other relationship because it is simple. Affairs are for self-indulgence and self-gratification. They are not created as a basis for building a lifetime relationship or for rearing children, nor do they work for those purposes.

If you are having an affair and want to continue, remember that it is temporary and don't build your life around it. Let it be a pleasure if you wish, but keep it compartmentalized.

I want to highlight the issue of STDs and HIV. I know it is hard to imagine that someone you care for could be diseased but they can. They may not even know they are, and even if they do, fewer than 50% tell their partner. This is a relevant issue. Please do not be naive; you cannot tell who has an STD, including HIV.

Men and women both have consequences from affairs, but women seem to pay the highest price because of childbearing. A woman who has children with a man who leaves her for another woman has a tremendous lifetime cost emotionally and financially. Another consequence exclusive to women is missing the opportunity to bear their own children. Often they wait for their lover to leave his marriage, and by the time they realize he is not going to marry them they are in their mid-30s and their chances of pregnancy have dropped severely.

Men initiate the majority of marriages and divorces. It is important to remember that the satisfaction level in one marriage is not much different than in the next. Marriage to a woman more than ten years younger has a good chance of ending in another divorce.

In my opinion, it is hard to argue that divorce is good for children. At its best, marriage teaches children how to get along with others, how to problem-solve and how to give and receive love.

Over and over I see people in second marriages learning what could have helped them in their first marriage. Everyone has something to learn about being a better partner.

PART 4

Advice for Spouses on Coping with an Affair

The realization of a spouse's affair transforms the otherwise unnoticed heartbeat into a feeling in your chest of a throbbing muscle on the verge of explosion. Your mind is flooded with questions. What does an affair mean about my marriage? What about our dreams and my future? What will I do? What can I do?

You are not a victim or a fool. There are several options for handling an affair, which are described in this section. Before you select one, be sure you clearly understand your goal. If your goal is to stay married, keep this thought in the foreground of all your decisions. If you want to divorce and you have children, remember that you will remain a co-parent the rest of your life.

The type of affair your spouse has affects its impact on your marriage. While sex affairs are hurtful and present health risks, they do not directly compete with a marriage relationship. A love affair is a threat to a marriage; the divorce rate among people who have love affairs is high. Divorce is not the only possible outcome, however. Marriages often become stronger having survived an affair because the spouses use the crisis to strengthen their commitment, remedy problems and deepen their understanding of one another's needs.

Before you decide which route to follow, read the next section to gain insight into what an affair does and does not mean about your marriage. Discovery of an affair is emotionally traumatic. This section also offers advice on how to cope physically and emotionally with that trauma.

▶ 13

Perspective

The type of affair your spouse is having is important. Sex affairs are disturbing and bring health risks into your marriage. Love affairs, in general, are a threat to a marriage, although most people who have loving affairs or bridge affairs do not want to end their marriage.

A few people become involved in one affair after another. Sometimes they are trying to meet a legitimate need but most of the time it is a neurotic compulsion that keeps them obsessed with new sexual partners.

In-love affairs are dangerous to the survival of the marriage. Drawing from my experience, I believe about 70% of in-love affairs destroy marriages. Even though affairees later regret their decision to leave the marriage, they are often determined to pursue their passion.

Sometimes people are self-absorbed and do not want to accept responsibility for their impact on others. There is not much chance of reasoning with these people. They will even argue that "Everyone gets divorced these days" or "It doesn't hurt children to go through a divorce. It makes them stronger and more realistic." They may tell you that you are better off without them because they don't love you anymore, as though their ability to love you was your choice, not theirs.

Unfortunately, their inability to negotiate does not bode well for their future relationships either. These people end up lonely and disappointed when the in-love feelings pass. Their new lover feels bitterly angry when he/she realizes the degree of their self-interest.

> "A few people are simply not good marriage partners and their affair is only a symptom of a much deeper problem."

Some spouses quickly opt for divorce once they know of an in-love affair. Others wait and see, and many do everything they can think of to bring their spouse back into the marriage. Whatever you do, take care of yourself. If you decide to try to save your marriage, do not allow your sense of self to be destroyed.

What an Affair Means About a Marriage

- ▸ An affair is a threat to any marriage.
- ▸ Most people report that their affair is about themselves, not about their marriage or their spouse.
- ▸ Affairs do impact spouses and families.
- ▸ Affairs are related to divorce, although rarely blamed for the divorce by the affairee.
- ▸ Affairs can be a reminder of the importance of marriage and family.
- ▸ An affair can be a crisis that provides an opportunity for improvement in yourself and in your marriage.

What Discovery of an Affair *Does Not* Mean about a Marriage

- ▸ Your spouse does not love you anymore.
- ▸ The marriage is over.
- ▸ The affair is over.
- ▸ The marriage will be the same as it was.
- ▸ It is the lover's fault.
- ▸ There is something wrong with someone, or this would not have happened.

▼ AFFAIREES MAY BE HAPPILY MARRIED

Some people, especially men, who are involved in affairs may consider themselves happy in their marriage. A 1992 survey by

CHART 44   **Percentage of Women and Men Who Are Happily Married When They Have an Affair**

Glass & Wright, 1985

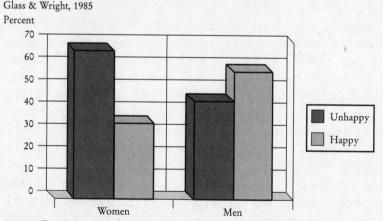

A man's affair does not indicate unhappiness with his marriage. Women are more often unhappy in their marriage when they have an affair.

Glass and Wright found that over half of the men and one-third of the women involved in affairs were happy in their marriages. About two-thirds of the women believed unhappiness in their marriage was part of the reason for their affairs. The remaining third said they were happy in their marriage and the affair was about themselves.

▼ WHAT LOVERS DO

Love affairs can begin by "just talking." Talking, listening, sharing secrets and self-disclosure are the cornerstones of love affairs. While making love is important to most affairees, it is only part of the attraction in long-term love affairs. What keeps the relationship going is an emotional connection.

Affairees commonly believe the affair enhances or subsidizes their marriages. Knowledge is power. Learn about affairs. The better informed you are, the more effective you can be at getting what you want. Here are some examples of what lovers do doing their affair.

Janice—"Kirk and I went to the same high school but I barely remember him from those years. We started seeing each other after our ten-year class reunion two years ago. At first we had mad, passionate sex nearly every day. Now we see each other a couple of times a week, sometimes for a 'breakfast meeting,' other times at lunch. We talk about our day, our families and our work in a way I don't talk to anyone else. We talk about our fears, our little successes and our feelings. I never worry about being criticized. We never criticize each other."

Kirk—"I remember Janice when she was a sweet kid of 16, a real doll. When we met again she had grown up. She was warm, friendly and fun. We spent a lot of time at our class reunion talking and she suggested we get together for lunch and finish catching up—so we did. Then we started having lunch every Wednesday. We talked like I had never talked to anyone before. We still talk a lot. We make love every chance we get. Sometimes it is really just sex—fast and fun. Other times, we spend hours. Once we spent a whole day making love."

Karen—"We talk about trivia, but we tell each other everything. Even secrets. We also laugh a lot. Dave is the funniest guy I have ever met. I love his wit. He keeps me in stitches with his jokes, his puns and his quick retorts. He has a funny story about even the most mundane experiences."

Dave—"We listen to each other without dividing our attention. In a way, we flatter each other, but the feelings are genuine. I really think she is terrific—sexy, fun and smart. I've always been a bit of a clown, so a lot of people don't take me very seriously. Karen is different. She loves my humor but also wants to know how I feel inside and what I think about things. She knows a serious, deeper side of me and lets me explore what I think and feel without judging me. We have a lot of sex play—pretending we are other people in other situations. Sometimes we dress up as characters, then undress, of course. We got the *Kama Sutra* books and tried all the positions. We laughed until it hurt."

As I listen to affairees, especially those who have love affairs, they have some common themes. Primarily the couple is focused on each other exclusively for the time; they listen, share and accept one another.

▼ ━━━━━━━━━━━━━━━━━━━━━━━━━━━

10 Features of Love Affairs
1. Sexual
2. Fun
3. Trusting
4. Accepting

5. Good humored
6. Warm
7. Affirming
8. Sensual
9. Experiential
10. Intense

▼ **DIVORCE AND AFFAIRS**

Emotional problems, including rejection, incompatibility and psychological distress, are blamed in over 40% of divorces. The second major category is sexual, including sexual problems between spouses, sexual dysfunction—and extramarital affairs.

CHART 45   **Primary Reasons for Divorce**

Janus, 1993

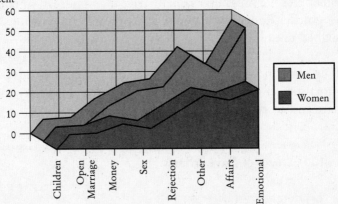

Emotional alienation is the major reason for divorce for both men and women. Affairs can be a reflection of the lack of emotional connection.

The Janus Report found that although 28% of married men and women had more than one extramarital affair without their marriage dissolving, 40% of divorced women and 45% of divorced men had extramarital sex more than once.

While some marriages are not destroyed by an affair, many others are. An affair is cited as the primary reason by 22% of women and 11% of men who divorce.

The fact that emotional issues rank number one as the major reason for divorce emphasizes the importance of continuous emotional involvement with one another that is both positive and intimate to keep your marriage strong.

▶ 14

Discovery: Options for Dealing with a Spouse's Affair

▼ DO YOU WANT TO KNOW?

A spouse may lie about an affair. If you believe your spouse is involved with someone else, use your senses.

▼
Telltale Signs of an Affair
- ▶ Loss of weight
- ▶ Change in hair
- ▶ Greater concern about clothing
- ▶ Passenger car seat adjustment
- ▶ New smells of soap or shampoo
- ▶ Use of breath mints
- ▶ Repeat number on cellular phone bill
- ▶ Extra key on key ring
- ▶ Restaurant matchbooks in pocket

- ▸ Lipstick or makeup on shirt
- ▸ Excuses to go out alone
- ▸ Vagueness regarding whereabouts
- ▸ More workouts
- ▸ Fresh-shower smell

▼ USE YOUR SENSES: LISTEN, LOOK, SMELL, FEEL

Listen— to your partner; does someone's name come up often in conversation?

Listen— for "little" lies or omissions.

Listen— for changes in comments about you, either more critical or more complimentary.

Look— for a change in appearance—sexier.

Look— for a different attitude—unusually cheerful or unusually irritable.

Look— at the family finances.

Smell— new colognes, perfumes.

Smell— breath freshened.

Smell— the scent of a lover.

Feel— emotional distance from your spouse.

Feel— emotional change in yourself.

Feel— tension.

▼ DISCOVERY

If you want to know, ask! If you don't—don't ask! If you decide to ask your spouse, prepare for a confrontation—with your spouse, with yourself and with your marriage.

CHART 46   **How an Affair Is Discovered by the Spouse**
Blumstein & Schwartz, 1983

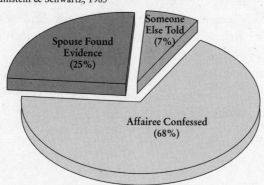

If an affair is discovered, it is often because the affairee confessed.

A 1983 survey found that about 68% of spouses were told of the affair by their mate. Most already suspected it. About 25% found some evidence and confronted their spouse, and about 7% were told by someone else. Only 10% were told without ever being suspicious.

Don't expect your spouse to fall on his or her knees, beg forgiveness, promise never to do it again and then live happily ever after with you. That only happens in old movies or with people who are good actors. If it happens to you, beware. It is too good to be true.

▼ OPTIONS FOR DEALING WITH THE SPOUSE'S AFFAIR

I am describing the options for coping with your spouse's affair early in this section so you will know you have choices. Think about these options as you read the subsequent chapters. This is an extremely difficult and complicated situation—there are no easy answers!

Affairs are often with co-workers. Most affairees do not intend to jeopardize their marriage, and a major deterrent to an affair is getting caught. About 50% of spouses find out about their partner's first affair. Some accept it; most just don't know what to do.

There are five basic strategies I have seen in dealing with a spouse's extramarital affair. They are acceptance, beating the competition, disappointing the lover, confrontation with the lover and confrontation with your spouse.

ACCEPTANCE

You have the option of simply ignoring the signs and signals of an affair. The reasons for taking this approach include:

- ▶ Not wanting a sexual relationship with the spouse, but wanting to maintain the marriage.
- ▶ Hoping the affair will dissolve or self-destruct.
- ▶ Sensing that the affair is helping the marriage.
- ▶ Covering up your own affair.
- ▶ Accepting infidelity as a lifestyle choice.

Larry simply decided to accept Helen's affair. He reasoned, "Helen and I have been married five years. I'm pretty sure she is having an affair and I know the guy. They travel for work together. Helen is a people person. She likes to party. I'm kind of shy and quiet. I adore Helen and love her very much but I also know I cannot keep her to myself or I'll lose her. Once we have kids I think she will settle down."

Occasionally people like Larry decide to ignore their spouse's affair because they do not view it as a threat to their marriage. Some people are angry, others are hurt, many are outraged, others just want to win their spouse back.

BEATING THE COMPETITION

If you want to beat the competition, analyze what you know about your spouse's needs and your marriage. Think about what your spouse is getting from the affair. Write both on a piece of paper. Select those needs you think are most important—that you can succeed at meeting. Then begin doing all you can to meet those needs.

▸ Since sex is likely to be part of the affair, invite more sex and try new things. Make it fun and add some adventure. Be a little daring.

▸ Be attentive to behaviors that irritate your spouse and work to change them.

▸ Create fun experiences.

▸ Send romantic cards to work.

▸ When he/she is away on business, send a card to the hotel.

▸ Send flowers or something visible to the office.

▸ When you call the office and speak to a secretary or co-worker, make positive comments about your spouse—emphasize that you are happily married.

▸ Have a good picture taken of the two of you having fun, or in a romantic embrace, then have it framed for the office.

▸ Spend more time with friends and family attending events and doing things that your spouse likes. During these times, talk about how fortunate you are to have such a good friend and lover in your spouse.

▸ Talk about how proud you are of your spouse, publicly and privately.

▸ Plan some romantic getaways for the two of you, and make sure friends, family and co-workers know about them.

▶ Rave about the wonderful, romantic time you had and how in love you are.

▶ Create date nights for the two of you, make them romantic—and sexual. Talk about these evenings openly.

Billie decided to take on her rival and beat the competition. "Duane and I had been married probably three years when I became suspicious that he was seeing someone else. I felt a little upset but not like I thought I would be. I sort of felt challenged in a way. My parents had been divorced and I had always blamed my mother for not being more attentive to my dad. I felt like I was doing the same thing. I wasn't usually home when Duane got home, because I liked to work out after work. We didn't usually have dinner together, because he liked to eat earlier than I. In fact, we didn't make love very often, because I stayed up later at night and he got up earlier in the morning.

"I decided I wasn't much of a wife to Duane the same as my mother hadn't been a good wife to my dad. I started thinking about what Duane wanted and needed from me and why he would be having an affair. It was not hard to figure out.

"I asked him one night if he felt I loved him. He laughed and said, 'You love your life and I'm part of providing that, so I guess you must love me.' Ouch! I asked if he was happy. We talked for a long time. He said he didn't want a divorce but he did feel lonely. I didn't bring up his affair, because I knew that might corner him or force a decision, or maybe I just didn't want to know for sure.

"Anyway, we decided to create more of the times we used to enjoy. He started bringing home flowers and he bought some CDs he thought I would like.

"I started getting up in the morning with him and went to work out then so we would get home about the same time at night. I mailed him an invitation at work to go for a weekend of 'lust and hedonism' to a little cabin we liked on the ocean. He loved it! I told his secretary how excited about the weekend we were and how much fun we had been having.

"I made more of an effort to stop by his office, take him a treat (we both work downtown) or call just to say I love you. Within a month there wasn't room for anyone else in his life nor was there any need. We were lovers again."

Billie's decision to beat the competition was made six years ago and she and Duane are still lovers. She focused on her marriage and what she knew about her husband's needs to change the direction their marriage was headed. Billie and Duane haven't stopped beating the competition.

Billie's insight into repeating her mother and father's relationship style and her decision to do something proactive probably saved her marriage. She could have confronted Duane or punished him but I doubt she'd have gotten the result she wanted. Billie used her intuitive sense of what worked with Duane. She knew he had a critical father and tended to become defiant if criticized. She was afraid confronting him would push him right into the arms of his lover.

It is important to think about how you want to handle a crisis as crucial as an affair. In Billie's case she thought about what she wanted. She wanted to be more involved in her marriage. She looked at what she knew about herself and her family background, and she thought about what she knew about Duane. She believed that he loved her and felt lonely and she knew he was reactive to criticism. She then chose a strategy that fit her style and ability. She became more of herself, especially the playful, loving side.

This strategy only works if the marriage isn't too far gone and there is still a desire in both partners to change the course of their marriage.

DISAPPOINTING THE LOVER

As in any part of life, sabotage is an option but can easily be seen as manipulative or controlling. If you decide on this strategy be sincere and loving.

You can create conflict between your spouse and his/her lover by making it necessary for them to change their dates. Nothing can ruin a romantic interlude like conflict or disappointment. Remember, lovers don't usually want to get caught.

▶ Change your weekend or evening plans at the last minute, so that the time you were planning to be out, you are home.

▶ Invite friends you both enjoy to join you spontaneously at an unusual time, such as a weekday evening or a weekend morning or lunch.

▶ Create the type of meals you know your spouse likes and be sure the two of you have dinner together frequently so the affairees won't be sharing romantic meals with one another.

▶ Since most affairs occur at home, mention that you may be able to stop home during the day.

▶ Get involved in your spouse's life, making him/her more aware of you and less available to the lover.

▶ Comment that your spouse's cologne or soap smells a little different.

▶ Borrow cash on the spur of the moment so that your spouse has less available without making a stop at the bank machine—which may make them late for their rendezvous. Lovers don't want to show evidence of their dates on credit cards.

▶ When your spouse offers to run an errand, offer to go along, but make it fun and positive. Talk about something *upbeat*—eliminate the time for a phone call to the lover.

▶ Call the office around 8:30, 11:45 or 4:30. Vary the time you call. Make the call warm, friendly, fun and brief. Call to tell a joke, or make romantic compliments. For example, "I was thinking about how great you are at . . ." or "I was remembering how much fun we had. . . ."

▶ Mention that you're checking charges and numbers on the cellular phone.

Calla decided to take aggressive action to sabotage Nelson's affair. She says, "The first time I saw Jamie, Nelson's new secretary, I thought she would be trouble. She was very cute and young; she was a '10.'

"When I joked with Nelson about how sexy Jamie was, he blew up. He said, 'I am working my butt off for you and the kids and all you can do is accuse me of being a liar and a cheat.' I thought, 'This approach is clearly going nowhere fast.' Maybe he was telling the truth, but when he started going to the office on weekends, I got nervous. I started making more 'couple' plans. We had gotten into the habit of going to so many kid events, we didn't plan anything else.

"We did some hiking, just the two of us, and took a picnic. I organized a cookout with friends, and we signed up for dancing lessons. I mentioned everything to his secretary and told her I hoped she could find someone who loved her as much as Nelson and I loved each other. I framed a picture for the office with him kissing me while I held our daughters. His secretary resigned a month later."

When women have affairs it is for an emotional connection, and they expect their lover to be loyal to them. Affairees tend to want to believe they are the only one who is really loved. When evidence mounts that the spouse is loved and enjoyed, the affair often loses some of its momentum.

CONFRONTATION WITH THE LOVER

Occasionally the spouse decides to meet the lover, usually with the hope of convincing the lover to leave. I have not seen this approach succeed in ending an affair.

A conflict with the lover may lead to a confrontation with the affairee, who may defend the lover—and force you both into an untimely and unwise decision.

I must forewarn you that I consider this a very risky strategy. Sometimes you can gain information from meeting the lover. You may get insight on what the motivation of the affair is or perhaps get a sense of its seriousness. If the goal is to gain information or understanding, meeting the lover may be useful. If the hope is to drive the lover away, it is a very remote possibility.

Kay and Simon had two small children under age 8 when she discovered Simon's affair. She found a love letter in his jeans pocket. When she confronted him with the letter, he just said, "I'm sorry. I didn't mean for this to happen but I'm in love with Janette and I can't seem to stop seeing her. I've tried five or six times but I always go back. It's worse than cocaine. I know what I am doing to you and the kids and I hate the person I have become." Then he sobbed, "But I can't let her go."

A week later, Kay took her children to Janette's office. Kay thought if Janette saw the children she would feel guilty about breaking up a family and she would let Simon go. Instead, Janette told Kay, in front of her children, that this wasn't Simon's first affair and that he had wanted to leave for a long time but had stayed because of the kids.

The kids started to cry, and Kay lost her temper and starting throwing things off Janette's desk. The security guards came and asked her to leave. When Simon found out what had happened he moved out.

Jeff had a similar experience when he decided to catch his wife, Lisa, in a lie. Jeff and Lisa had been married sixteen years. They were high school sweethearts and married right out of college. Jeff had had an affair once early in their marriage so he knew the signs—coming home late, hanging up the telephone when he came in the room, running to the grocery store at odd times, new clothes, new hairstyle, the works. He asked Lisa what was going on and she said she was just happy, nothing more, and that she loved him and he was being silly. She reminded him, "I have never been that interested in sex. Why would I go out of my way for it?"

Jeff recounts, "I tried to believe her but one day I decided to follow her. I expected her to meet her lover at the end of the day but she didn't and I was relieved. I was beginning to think I was being silly until one day she forgot her watch and I thought I would take it to her office. She wasn't there. The next three mornings I followed her. The first two mornings she went straight to work but the third morning she got off the freeway two exits early and pulled up to a little roadside restaurant/motel. My heart was pounding but I was hoping she was just meeting someone for breakfast so I watched. She didn't go to the restaurant door. Instead she went up the outside staircase and walked into room #8. I drove away in horror. Then I went back and watched when she left. I waited for her lover and watched him get into his car. I felt numb. Then I followed him to work.

"I didn't know what to do. So I sat there all day just looking at the building Lisa's lover, Terry, worked in. At the end of the day, as he left the building, I got out of my car and stopped him.

"I said, 'I'm Lisa's husband and I want to know what is going on. I followed her to the motel this morning.' Terry said, 'Well, I guess you know then. Lisa and I met two years ago and we have been seeing each other every Thursday morning and

Saturday afternoon. I'm not interested in marriage and I'm not trying to break up your marriage. That's between you and Lisa. Lisa started this affair because she said you were a lousy lover and she didn't want to spend the rest of her life without good sex.'

"Somewhat dazed, I went home. Lisa knew immediately. I couldn't think. I wanted to hurt her and I wanted to beg her to forget Terry and just love me. I heard her talking but I couldn't really listen. Then I grabbed her and shook her, then I pushed her, I guess. By then our daughter was screaming, 'Daddy, don't. What's wrong with you? Go away, Daddy. Don't hurt Mommy.' I got ahold of myself hearing my daughter's cries.

"It was a nightmare none of us will forget. Playing private eye sure didn't solve anything. In the end Lisa said she had only seen Terry for about six months, not two years. We put it back together, but I wish I had never talked to Terry and that night from hell had never happened."

Spying on one another is not a good choice even though affairees lie when questioned about a possible affair. I have never seen that confronting the lover works out in any productive way. As in Terry's experience, it results in confusion, rage and violence. Direct confrontation with your spouse, while difficult, is a much better choice.

CONFRONTATION WITH YOUR SPOUSE

Deciding to confront your spouse means gathering information first. Collect evidence so that your spouse knows you know and does not attempt to lie or deceive you. Lying can be more damaging than the affair itself. Do *not* use this situation to test your spouse's honesty.

When you are ready to talk about your suspicions with your spouse, keep the focus on your spouse, yourself and your marriage. Minimize the importance of the lover by giving little attention to who, where and when. You cannot do anything about the past and you do not want your spouse to start defending their lover.

Talk about your feelings, what you want and what each of you can do now. If your spouse tells you they want to stay married—believe it. Healthy confrontation requires preparation, good communication skills and emotional clarity.

Be ready to listen . . . carefully, thoughtfully, patiently, like a friend.

How to Ask

- ▶ Be prepared for a shock.

- ▶ Think about what you want. Do you want to rebuild this relationship or end it? Behave accordingly.

- ▶ Choose a place that is private and where you will not be interrupted.

- ▶ Choose a time when neither of you is tired or angry.

- ▶ Do not drink alcohol—keep a clear mind.

- ▶ Use your best communication skills.

Do Not . . .

- ▶ *Do not* threaten: "I am leaving," "Get out," or "Choose now."

- ▶ *Do not* attack, accuse or indict.

- ▶ *Do not* do all the talking.

- ▸ *Do not* blame yourself or develop excuses for either of you.

- ▸ *Do not* communicate damaging, hurtful or threatening feelings to punish your spouse.

- ▸ *Do not* think you will resolve the problems during your first talk or any time soon. You are just beginning to learn about and understand one another differently than you have in the past.

Jason and Ariel had been married eighteen years when Jason became suspicious that she was involved with someone else. He looked for evidence and found a number on their cellular phone bill that was called repeatedly. He looked on the Mastercard bill and found numerous restaurant charges on evenings when she was out of town or at a meeting. Then one evening he picked up the phone while they were talking. "I'd heard enough," he says. "I was pretty upset but I waited until after the kids went to bed. I suggested we talk in the living room. I told her what I had heard on the telephone. She didn't deny it.

"She said she did not want to break up our marriage, but that I was never home. She started talking about all my problems. First, I didn't talk to her enough. I didn't really know her because I was too busy. Secondly, she said we didn't have fun anymore. It was bad. I mustered all my discipline not to criticize her, too. Instead, I insisted I loved her and said, 'Ariel, I agree our marriage needs work, every relationship needs work. We made a commitment to each other when we married and again when we had children. We both need to figure out how to make this work. It isn't just about you and me.'

"She said, 'I don't know about us, but I don't want to break up our family. I'll go to counseling separately or with you. I know an affair was not the right way to handle my loneliness but I also know I don't want to feel as alone as I did.' "

After they had been in counseling for a couple of months, Ariel started talking to Jason. She told him about the affair and why she thought she had gotten into it in the first place. She took responsibility for her choice of pursuing a new relationship rather than talking to him about her issues. She had felt she was getting older, nearing 38, and that she was no longer sexually attractive to him. She confessed, "When someone else showed an interest in me, I didn't resist, thinking initially I was just flirting. But one thing led to another and pretty soon I was engulfed in an affair."

She told Jason she still cared for him and wanted more of him in their marriage, not less. They started talking about how to rebuild the trust and intimacy in their marriage.

When Jason confronted Ariel he chose a time and place that was quiet and private. He stayed focused on their marriage rather than on Ariel's affair. He let Ariel talk and he managed to listen without becoming defensive. When their confrontation calmed down, he reminded Ariel of what they both wanted, an intact family.

It has taken two years for Ariel and Jason to build an intimate marriage. Both had to learn to communicate in ways that brought them closer. They had a strong commitment to their marriage and their children and they were determined not to get divorced. Over time they created a new and better marriage.

In contrast, Leesa's confrontation with Neil went in exactly the direction she had most feared—it became a cruel screaming match. Leesa explains, "Neil and I had been married twenty years when our friend Beth and her husband, Roger, became a major presence in our lives. It began to seem as though all our plans and conversations centered on Roger and Beth.

"I began to notice that when we all got together either Neil or Beth had to go to the grocery store and during the same time the other would disappear.

"I wanted to ignore the signs, but I knew. I told Neil I wanted to talk and not to make other plans. I had a glass of wine. I told him I knew about his relationship with Beth and he had to stop it.

"He said he didn't want a divorce, but he wouldn't quit seeing her, either. I thought I would die—this was my worst nightmare. He said he would leave, he needed some time, we could just separate. I screamed, 'No, you can't!' I called him names and threatened him in every way I could think of. I said, 'You have always been a loser. My dad didn't want me to marry you, even your mother said you needed help. Our friends wonder why I married you; they make fun of you because you do so many stupid things.'

"Neil yelled back, 'If you weren't such a snob, always sucking up to other people, you might be able to keep a husband. But no, you have to be out brown-nosing. You're selfish. You aren't even a good mother and you're a lousy lay.'

"We went on like that for hours. I didn't want him to leave, but how could I live with him while he was screwing my friend. This was like a soap opera, only it was my life.

"I couldn't stop him from seeing her and I did not want him to leave. I started telling him that she had other lovers and everyone knew she was looking for someone with money. I could see him get stone cold. I told him to get out and that I never wanted to see him again.

"I went upstairs and woke up the kids and told them their dad was leaving us to be with his mistress, Beth. They cried and Neil left.

"Neil and I are still separated but we go to counseling and we are talking in ways we never have before. Beth stayed with

Roger in a sexless marriage, which I think surprised and hurt Neil. We don't see them anymore.

"I think I have to let go of Neil, which is the hardest thing I have ever done. That night was such a mistake. Neither of us can forget the things we said to each other."

Leesa is right. You can't take back the things you say. Cruel, hurtful words are hard to forget even if you can forgive. When you confront your spouse, don't inflict more pain on each other. Stay focused on your marriage and what you want. If your conversation is going the wrong way, stop and try again later.

▼ KNOWING WHEN TO QUIT

Reason does not always prevail in life, love or infidelity. Some affairees are determined to end their marriage and you cannot stop them. It is hard to know when to quit trying to save your marriage. Following are the signs I think should alert you to the possibility that you may have to let go:

- ▶ When your sense of self is being depreciated by ongoing contact with your spouse.
- ▶ When the relationship is physically or emotionally abusive.
- ▶ When your spouse is unable or unwilling to love.

Austin met Sundie at a conference and they had been meeting monthly at various resorts around the country for nearly a year before Austin told his wife, Conni, he was divorcing her.

Austin had a reputation with acquaintances and colleagues for being arrogant and volatile. He had no friends. Conni pleaded with Austin to give her some time. He moved to their guest bedroom but he seldom spoke to her and called his affairee in front of her, professing his love and devotion.

Conni went to counseling, lost fifteen pounds and tried desperately to change anything about herself she thought Austin didn't like. Austin mimicked and ridiculed her efforts.

He would say he'd be home for dinner with their children then not show up. He promised to take the kids swimming one afternoon but then changed his mind. The kids were devastated. The same pattern occurred with everyone. Conni finally decided to give up when Austin forgot to pick up one of their kids from sports. She realized his selfishness, anger and lies were damaging to her and her children.

The divorce was ugly because Austin thought everything should be his and he would just pay the bills he thought appropriate. Through the divorce Conni could see clearly that Austin did not love anyone and their marriage could never have been healthy.

Discovering a spouse's affair is traumatic. It feels like a tragedy—and yet it may not be a tragedy at all, given time. Upon discovering an affair, commit time and energy to caring for yourself and making thoughtful choices. When confronting a problem of this magnitude, be sure you are functioning at your best. Read the following chapter on maintaining your physical and emotional health during this extraordinarily stressful period.

Think about your long-term goal. If your goal is to maintain the marriage and improve it, start now. You can accept the affair, beat the competition, disappoint the lover, confront the lover or confront your spouse. Many marriages become more realistic and gratifying to both spouses after an affair. Stay focused and determined.

▼ **ALWAYS REMEMBER...**

Negotiate for What You Want

▸ I love you and I want to understand what happened.
▸ I want you to stop seeing your lover.
▸ I want to stay married to you.

Do Not Threaten or Insult

▸ Get out, I never want to see you again.
▸ I'll tell everyone—the kids, your parents, etc.
▸ I never did trust you!
▸ Your lover is a moron, etc.

▸ 15

Coping with the Shock and Trauma

Discovery of an affair is extremely difficult for both spouses. Even when you suspect that your mate might be having an affair, finding out is traumatic.

This is a crisis! During this time it is essential that you maintain a clear mind, good health and a realistic perspective. I have gone into detail in this chapter on how to cope with the shock of discovery of an affair because I have seen many people become so frantic, frightened and desperate that they created exactly the outcome they did not want. Take time to decide what you want, take care of yourself and keep the door to communication open.

The feeling of shock may actually have physical effects ranging from headaches and backaches to higher blood pressure.

Care for yourself as though you have been injured—you have!

▼ COPING WITH THE CRISIS TOGETHER OR SEPARATELY

Discovery of an extramarital affair is a shock, physically and emotionally. The sense of shock occurs for both spouse and affairee. Both partners find themselves embroiled in distress. An important focus during the shock stage is maintaining good physical and mental health. Numerous recent studies have made it clear that strong interpersonal support, good nutrition, exercise and meditation help during times of acute stress. Important decisions will be made and it is crucial that you be operating at your best.

The discovery of an affair provides the opportunity to help one another heal from the pain, the shame and the fear. It is also a time for tremendous personal and interpersonal growth.

Brandon vividly recalls the Saturday afternoon when Marie told him she had a lover. He says, "When Marie started saying she had gotten involved in a relationship I felt confused. 'What is she talking about?' I wondered. Then the lights went on as she said it was just an infatuation. She was talking about a lover—having an affair. I couldn't believe it—not my Marie. I wanted her to keep talking. I wanted to know everything—Who? Why? What did you do?—but I didn't want to hear any of it.

"I just grabbed her and held her as tight as I could. I didn't want to ever let her go. We both cried and held each other all night."

Marie cries as she recalls their conversation, "I was nervous about telling Brandon but Reed was starting to call me at work, at home and on my cell phone. I didn't want Brandon to hear about this affair from someone else.

"So I started by saying, laughingly, 'I kind of made a big mistake.' He chuckled and said, 'OK, Marie, what big mistake did you make, my dear?' I started to explain that it was a relationship I had gotten into without thinking. Brandon looked puzzled as I went on to say that it had just been an infatuation. Then I could see from the disbelief on his face that he understood what I was saying.

"I have never seen such agony in anyone's face. He said, 'No, not you, Marie.' He paused, struggling to breathe, then said, 'Tell me everything—Who? Why? What did you do?'

"I have never hated myself so much or felt so much shame from hurting this wonderful man. I kept saying, 'I'm so sorry.' It seemed so trite but I couldn't think of what to say or do.

"He reached for me and for a moment I thought maybe he would hit me. I guess I hoped he would but he didn't, he just grabbed me, held me and whimpered, 'I don't want to ever let you go. I'll love you better and stay closer. Don't leave me again.' We both cried all night."

Brandon's reaction to Marie showed her the depth of his love for her and the strength of his character. As they talked, neither blamed the other and both searched for understanding. They agreed that Brandon could ask about the affair any time he wanted to talk about it but they wouldn't discuss any explicit sexual contact she had. Brandon knew it was painful for Marie to talk about her affair and he appreciated her willingness. They talked about the type of marriage that would be ideal and started working together to create it. They treated each other as though they had been in a bad accident and both were tender and bruised.

Two years after their affair crisis they are happier than ever. Each credits the other for their hard work and determination in creating a healthy, intimate marriage.

▼ Emotional Stress

The body responds to stress with a series of neurochemical responses known as the "fight-or-flight" response. The brain and the heart are connected through nerves, called the sympathetic nervous system. When your brain receives a threat message, it signals the body to prepare by producing stress hormones such as adrenaline and steroids such as cortisol. Your body becomes able to do physical battle. When physical confrontation follows, the body's reaction is appropriate. When this stage of readiness for battle continues and stress becomes chronic, it is dangerous.

It is frightening to find sudden changes in the way your body functions. Amanda was spending so much time in the bathroom she was convinced she had colon cancer. Fortunately, she didn't. It was just one way her body reacted to stress. Recognize and manage your stress by taking exceptionally good care of yourself. *Resist the fight-or-flight impulse!*

CHART 47

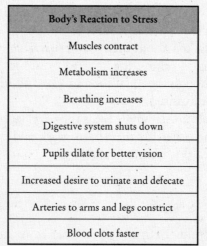

Body's Reaction to Stress
Muscles contract
Metabolism increases
Breathing increases
Digestive system shuts down
Pupils dilate for better vision
Increased desire to urinate and defecate
Arteries to arms and legs constrict
Blood clots faster

▼ TAKE TIME

It is tempting to think you should do something to solve this, right now. The impulse may be to strike back, blame or collapse in a heap. These reactions create defensive responses and will drive your spouse away. Threats and accusations often take the relationship in a direction neither of you would choose.

It may be tempting to react with rejection in order to teach a lesson, but this tactic is bound to backfire. Acting on impulse, getting even or making intimidating threats does not create closeness. If you want comfort and affection, express those desires warmly and softly. When you are glad to see your spouse—smile broadly. Behave as though your spouse is your friend. Although this may be the most difficult time in your life, your spouse is not your enemy.

▼ GOOD HEALTH IS ESSENTIAL

Good health is important all the time, but it is particularly important during times of acute stress and when important decisions are being made. There will be days you do not feel like doing anything, including exercising, eating well and being around other people, but do it anyway. Treat yourself as though you are recovering from an injury—you are!

Studies from Yale and Harvard show that the greatest risk of illness comes when people believe they have little or no control over their lives. During this time of crisis there are things you can do to help yourself, both physically and emotionally.

Remember, this is a crisis and you need to make an extra effort to care for yourself and to manage the intense stress you are experiencing.

Carmen says, "I thought I would lose my mind when Mac moved out. He kept saying he needed time. I felt like I was 'on hold' waiting for him to decide between me or her. It was a terrible feeling. I started hating him and hating myself for being so passive. I thought, 'I'll file for divorce. I just have to do something—I won't just wait around.'

"Then I realized this whole thing had exploded just a month ago. It seemed like an eternity but it wasn't. I needed time, too. Speeding toward a divorce neither of us wanted made no sense rationally, but I had to do something.

"I started doing everything I could think of, ranging from French lessons, horseback riding, meditation, cooking classes and exercise. French lessons didn't work because my memory was so bad, cooking classes made me sad because Mac wasn't here to cook for, horseback riding left me feeling lonely. Exercise and meditation were best for me. I could keep busy, have a sense of control over my life, and I could see how I was able to change when I worked at it. I did a lot of reading, especially on communication, and realized my style of communicating was loaded with blame and criticism and that I seldom asked for what I wanted. I worked hard to learn and I liked that in myself. I had discipline and determination."

Like Carmen, most people find it difficult to just wait. You can only change the things you have the power to control. While personalities do not change, you can change your interpersonal style, self-talk and level of skill. Forcing a relationship decision doesn't work. You cannot change someone else, you can only change yourself.

Health Goals

- ▸ Exercise.
- ▸ Meditate.
- ▸ Learn to express feelings.
- ▸ Follow a healthy nutrition plan.

- ▶ Be involved with other people.
- ▶ Get help/counseling if necessary.
- ▶ Read books that give you perspective or teach you new skills.
- ▶ Read for pleasure and escape.

▼ SHOCK

When threatened, our instincts lead us to fight-or-flight, but when it comes to saving a marriage, use your mind as well as your heart. Take a deep breath. Feel your pain, your love and your fear. Think about what is right in your marriage, not just the mistakes. The choices you make now will set a course for your life. Although there is a drive to do something quickly, don't. Take time to adjust to the trauma and shock.

Ordinary life tasks may feel overwhelming. Driving is hazardous, drinking is dangerous, self-medication is risky. The ability to concentrate may be diminished, sleep patterns disrupted and judgment impaired. It is common to forget what you were doing in the middle of a simple task or get lost on the way home. An idea that sounds reasonable today may seem ridiculous later. These are all normal responses to extreme stress.

Remember

- ▶ This is a traumatic and stressful experience.
- ▶ Do not make major decisions now.
    - –Don't change jobs.
    - –Don't quit or start work.
    - –Don't take a long vacation.
- ▶ Do not use alcohol to feel better.
- ▶ Do not medicate yourself!

▼ SOCIAL HEALTH

Getting involved with others meets basic health needs and helps you to get beyond a preoccupation with yourself. You may feel tempted to withdraw to hide your pain, but isolation is dangerous. You are a social creature, and contact with others is necessary for your emotional well-being.

The absence of emotionally intimate contact with another person has repeatedly been linked to poor health. *You need contact with other people!*

FIND SUPPORT FOR YOURSELF

Seek support. Do not ask for advice from friends. Ask for the opportunity to share feelings, cry, vent anger, explain the disbelief and express the hurt. Depend on friends for comfort, companionship, feedback and reassurance but not for advice. Good advice in one situation can be bad advice in another.

Be discreet. Everyone has an opinion about what they would or would not do. Many people have a pat answer: "I would not put up with that" or "Throw him out, then he will see." Some who have been through this type of marital crisis will have their own solutions. The fact is, they do *not* know the answer that's best for you.

Talk about feelings and experiences, but try not to build a case. Do not encourage friends to analyze or criticize your spouse. This dynamic is damaging to rebuilding your marriage and may ultimately destroy your friendship.

If you need to explode, then find a counselor, play racquetball or write letters you don't send—but don't inflict your rage on friends, family or spouse.

Make specific requests. If you want to talk to a friend, say so. If you just want to be with someone—ask. Sometimes simple companionship is enough, but friends will not know unless you tell them. Sometimes you must accept no for an answer, without making it rejection! You will be especially sensitive during this time. Stay close to the people who care about you.

Emma lost a relationship with one of her best friends, Annette, when she confided that her husband, Nathan, was having an affair. Emma was vehement that she was finished with Nathan—that she could never forgive him. Annette agreed and told others how despicable Nathan was. Annette agreed that Emma should kick Nathan out of the house and teach him a lesson. Annette and Emma spent hours talking about all that was wrong with Nathan. When Emma reconciled with Nathan, Annette thought Emma was a fool. She also felt betrayed by Emma because of all the energy she had spent supporting Emma's decision to separate, and she didn't want her husband to think he could get away with an affair. Nathan and Emma worked through the problems created by the affair, but Emma and Annette's relationship did not survive.

Consider seeing a counselor who can listen with care and concern and who can give you perspective, teach you new skills and help you through this difficult time.

▼ ALTRUISM

Another way of looking out for yourself is to look out for others. You can become consumed with yourself and your problems. Get some distance—and get your mind off yourself now and then.

Altruism is consideration of other people without thought of yourself. It is based on understanding and acceptance and it requires a sense of compassion and empathy. During this crisis, balance self-awareness with concern and involvement with others. Helping others gives us perspective on our own problems, plus better physical and emotional health.

"Altruism, compassion and forgiveness—opening your
heart—can be a powerful means of healing the isolation that
leads to stress, suffering and illness."

—DEAN ORNISH, M.D.

▼ NUTRITION

During this crisis, eating patterns can be affected. Be conscientious about eating healthy foods regularly. Your mind and
body are already stressed, so be sure you are supplying yourself with the needed nutrients to maintain your physical and
emotional stamina.

Acute stress usually affects eating. Some people overeat;
others stop eating. Dierdra felt sick every time she thought of
Philip making love to someone else. She says, "I feel sick to my
stomach all the time. I have no appetite. Nothing sounds good
to me. I lost fifteen pounds in two weeks and even the kids
started telling me to eat something. I am making myself sit
down and eat with the kids. I fix simple things and eat small
amounts, but I stopped losing weight."

Esther had the opposite reaction. She says, "I eat constantly. I feel hungry all the time. No matter what or how often I
eat, I feel hungry." She decided to start a weight reduction class
and signed up for golf lessons so she would get more exercise.

▼ EXERCISE

One of the most important tools in controlling stress and
maintaining health is exercise. Structured exercise and exercise
included in a daily routine both produce endorphins, which
help you feel happier. Avoid depression and fatigue during this
highly stressful time by developing an unusually intense level
of exercise.

Eddy found that running helped him. He says, "I just didn't have any energy and I felt no interest in sports for the first time in my life. I knew I better get moving. I make it a point to run every other day for two miles. I also look for ways to get exercise. I take the stairs at work instead of the elevator and I park away from the store when I run errands. Every little bit helps."

▼ COMMUNICATE EMOTIONS

Develop an emotional vocabulary. Learn feeling words. Use "I" statements and take responsibility for your own feelings. For example, "I feel so hurt, I could die," not "You are killing me." Do it without blame or vengeance. If you don't know how, learn how. Read, take classes, go to seminars, see a counselor and start immediately.

Expressing feelings is healthy, and there should be a variety of feelings, not just one or two. One feeling, often hurt or anger, can become a favorite. Overexpression of any feeling generates more of that feeling. For example, repeatedly expressing anger makes you angrier, and recurrent feelings of hurt make you feel more hurt. Both anger and hurt ultimately drive people away from you if they are not resolved.

Be sure expressing your feelings is taking you toward resolution not repetition.

THOUGHTS ARE DIFFERENT FROM FEELINGS

Feelings are true, they are real, and they are based in the present. No one can legitimately argue that a person doesn't feel what they feel. Feelings are the basis for intimacy and understanding. They can be more influential and intimate than thoughts.

Thoughts are often judgments and sometimes criticisms. They are often based in the past or projected into the future. Thoughts are in an intellectual rather than an emotional language.

If the goal is to have an intellectual communication, thoughts are valuable and helpful. If the goal is intimacy or understanding, feelings and information are best. Feelings enhance intimacy.

A simple test to distinguish a thought from a feeling is to say aloud, "I think . . . anger, fear, love, joy, etc." If it just doesn't sound right, experiment.

Feelings, thoughts and judgments each play a valuable role in your dealings with one another. They each have a different purpose and a different impact.

Owning Your Feelings

1. Take time on a daily basis just to feel.
2. Become familiar with the names of feelings.
3. Learn about your feelings.
4. Express feelings verbally, physically or in writing.

Feelings

I feel—angry, scared, confused, worried, delighted, furious, resentful, jealous, envious, optimistic, joyous, guilty, pained, trapped, disgusted, excited, silly, naughty, clever, confident, curious, surprised, challenged, threatened, ecstatic, euphoric, anxious, desperate.

Thoughts Disguised as Feelings

I feel—that I am right, that I was hurt, that you should . . .

Judgments Disguised as Feelings

I feel—that you are trying to make me ..., that you are always ..., that I never ..., that I know ...

FEEL AND EXPRESS A RANGE OF EMOTIONS

The desire to rant and rave and bring up every bit of rage is tempting. The betrayal seems to deserve the greatest punishment imaginable. Anger is a normal response to an affair and should be expressed. However, raging anger by itself is damaging, not healing. Allow yourself to feel a variety of feelings, not just one or two. Express your feelings and make sure they are balanced. If your feelings have a very limited range or are muted, consider whether you may be depressed.

Express the right feeling in the right tone. Hurt should sound like hurt, fear like fear and so forth. Hurt expressed as anger drives the listener away. When the hurt is communicated as hurt, it invites the listener closer and elicits comfort and reassurance. Be sure that what you say sounds like what you feel. Remember, anger by itself is not healing.

▼ PERCEPTION DETERMINES REALITY

Much stress and unhappiness comes not from what happens but from perceptions surrounding these events. An affair, or any other marriage crisis, is not the end of your life. It may even be the beginning of something good.

The marriages that are most likely to end because of an affair are those in which the spouse believes that an affair means the end of the marriage. Bad things happen in everyone's life. You have power within yourself to make good choices—even in a bad situation.

"Real power is ours already when we stop giving it away. Real happiness is ours already when we stop believing it's something we have to get from the outside. Real peace is already ours when we stop disturbing ourselves. Real freedom is ours already when we stop limiting ourselves."
—DEAN ORNISH, M.D.

We Have the Ability to Turn Fears into Truths

▶ Fear of being hurt creates distance and defensive responses, does not allow intimacy and results in isolation, then hurt.

▶ Fear of abandonment creates suspicion and jealousy, making others hide their normal doubts and disappointments, and eventually results in abandonment.

▶ Believing an affair is the end of marriage often makes it so.

▶ Our perceptions determine how we react to a situation, and often our perceptions are wrong.

▶ Stress comes with life; it is how we interact with it that determines the outcome.

▼ DEPRESSION

Depression occurs during times of crisis or change. Studies show that 30% of people experience enough depression to seek medical attention.

Symptoms of depression can be dramatic, such as uncontrollable crying or anger, or they can be subtle, like "not much energy." Sleep irregularity, especially early morning awakening; appetite or weight changes; aches and pains (backache and headache); and respiratory difficulty are all symptomatic of depression. Depression is a biochemical imbalance in the brain and it runs in families. Anxiety frequently accompanies depression.

Any depression that lasts longer than a month should be treated with counseling and/or an antidepressant medication so that it does not become chronic. Antidepressants are effective for 70% of people who have depression lasting more than a couple of weeks.

Antidepressants act on one or both of two neurotransmitter systems: the serotonergic system (which uses serotonin as a transmitter) and the noradrenergic system (which uses norepinephrine). These drugs block the reuptake of the neurotransmitters, affecting a variety of functions such as mood, sexual arousal, appetite and sleep.

Antidepressants are not addictive, but they are serious medications and should be used only under the supervision of a physician. All antidepressant medications have some potential side effects, but they can be managed. If one medication does not work, try another. You can find one that will help you. Counseling is also helpful with depression. In a 1996 article in the *New York Times*, Cognitive Therapy is reported to be the most effective form of therapy in treating depression.

Symptoms of Depression

- ▶ Sleeping too much or too little
- ▶ Low energy or chronic tired feeling
- ▶ Feelings of inadequacy, loss of self-esteem
- ▶ Less effectiveness or productivity
- ▶ Less ability to concentrate or think clearly
- ▶ Social withdrawal
- ▶ Lack of interest in pleasurable activities
- ▶ Irritability or excessive anger
- ▶ Unresponsiveness to praise or rewards

- ► Less activity or talkativeness
- ► Pessimistic attitude about the future
- ► Feeling sorry for oneself
- ► Crying easily and frequently
- ► Repeated thoughts of death or suicide

The presence of three or more of these symptoms indicates possible depression.

▼ COUNSELING

Counseling is an option for coping with an affair, understanding yourself and your spouse and learning new relationship skills. Select a counselor who will help you recognize and vent feelings, as well as provide information and resources. The credentials of a therapist are often less important than how you feel about the person.

There are several credentials for people who do counseling, therapy, psychotherapy or psychoanalysis, all of which can be referred to as "therapy." Psychiatrists, who are medical doctors, and clinical psychologists, who have Ph.D. degrees, usually practice psychotherapy. Counselors and therapists usually have a master's or doctoral degree in psychology or social work and are often more oriented toward teaching skills and new ways of looking at problems. The credentials of the therapist do not necessarily reflect their style. Some therapists listen and coach, while others give advice.

Ask friends, clergy or a physician for a referral and interview several therapists. Ask about their rates and their philosophy. Your needs may change during the course of the marriage crisis. Some therapists will not see you for individual counseling once they have seen you as a couple, while others will. Sometimes it is important to have your own therapist during a crisis, sometimes not. It is perfectly acceptable to change therapists.

Be sure that the focus of the counseling is on you. It is often more comfortable to figure out what is wrong with the spouse or speculate on his or her "real" problem. Avoid slogans, like "She is afraid of intimacy" or "This is a mid-life crisis." These are useless clichés that deflect shared responsibility. It may be painful to see mistakes honestly, but it is also empowering!

▼

How to Find Support

1. Select a friend in whom you have trust and confidence. Tell them you need to talk confidentially without criticism or advice.
2. Ask your friends, physicians or clergy for the names of several counselors. Call several therapists and arrange to meet with each of them until you find someone you like. Although a fee will be charged for each session, it is important to find the right counselor. Select someone you like who shares your values.
3. Call the local mental health agency and ask for information on support groups in your area.

▼ MEDITATION

Meditation allows you the opportunity to feel, experience and know yourself. Take time to listen to your inner self. It is important.

First, find a quiet and tranquil place where you can sit peacefully and relax for twenty or thirty minutes.

Next, relax, close your eyes and feel yourself breathing. Let the tension in your muscles leave your body. Concentrate on the rise and fall of your tummy with each breath. Focus your mind on feeling and counting each breath as a gentle breeze coming in through your nose and a gentle breeze flowing out of your mouth. Exclude all other thoughts and feelings.

Some people find it easier to focus on an object than on breathing. You can use a symbol, a flickering flame or mantra. It doesn't matter, the goal is to clear your mind of thoughts and allow yourself to center within yourself.

In the beginning you will find that your mind wanders but with practice you will be able to stay focused. Meditation focuses your mind on the present, and brings you strength and power. A good description of meditation techniques can be found in *The Book of Stress Survival* by Alix Kirsta.

▼ Maintaining Social Health

- ▸ A sense of isolation leads to chronic stress and often to illness.

- ▸ Intimacy and feelings of connection help healing.

- ▸ Remember: talk about feelings and experiences, but try not to build a case. Do not encourage friends to analyze or criticize your spouse.

When Liz and Hal separated, Liz wanted to disappear. She even wished she could just die, but instead she learned how to love and care for herself. She grimaces as she starts to tell her story: "Hal and I seemed to be arguing constantly, which wasn't really typical of us. He started criticizing how I looked—my weight, my hair, my clothes. He said mean things, like 'You look ten years older than you are.'

"It seemed like he criticized whatever I did. If I made dinner he would say, 'Don't you know how to make anything but pasta? The kids need fruit, vegetables and protein.' So I would get fruit and vegetables. Then he would say, 'Can't we sit down and eat together?' I just couldn't win.

"I bought a new dress and he said, 'There is no use wasting money on clothes when you don't take care of yourself.' He went on, 'When are you going to clean this house? It looks like pigs live here.' One Saturday afternoon he said he was taking the kids over to his sister's, and we needed to talk. When he came back he said he wanted a divorce. I immediately accused him of having someone else. He said, 'It doesn't matter. I don't want you the way you are.'

"Finally he admitted there was someone else but she wasn't the reason. I started yelling and swearing at him. I told him to get out. He left.

"I was truly in shock. I just sat there the rest of the night looking out the window. The next day Hal called and asked me how I was doing. I begged him to come back. So he came over and we talked. I begged him not to leave, but he said, 'No, I can't live like this.' He brought the kids home and he told them we were separating for a while. He would live at home in the guest room for a month; then he would move to a place of his own.

"I just watched and listened. I was immobilized. He did as he said. He stayed a month, then got an apartment. I just kept eating. I could hardly take care of the kids. I couldn't sleep at night. I didn't want to get up in the morning.

"One day I saw an old friend in the grocery store and I hurried around the aisle to hide. When I got into the car I looked in the mirror and said, 'Who are you?' I used to have lots of friends, I played tennis, I volunteered for the arts. I was happy. What had happened to me? I finally got the nerve to call a friend who had gone to counseling and asked for the therapist's name and phone number. I called right away before I could change my mind.

"In counseling I started to look at myself inside and out. My counselor thought I was depressed and recommended a change in my diet and exercise and an antidepressant. It reminded me of Hal's criticisms. I said I would try exercise and diet first. If I didn't feel better I would take the medication. I tried to exercise, but days went by and I just couldn't get going, so I went on Prozac.

"I couldn't even tell I was taking it. But it did make a difference. I just didn't feel so empty and lifeless. I started exercising half an hour every day, walking mostly. I practiced feeling my feelings, and if I didn't like what I was feeling I thought about what I could do to change. The kids noticed the difference, saying, 'You seem happy, Mom. Dad must be doing something, is he coming home?' I was struck by the accuracy of their comment. I had made Hal responsible for how I felt, how I looked and what I did.

"I signed up for a fitness club, something I thought I would never do. I met with a personal trainer and a dietitian who worked out a program for me. In a month I had lost nine pounds but, more important, I felt good.

"I decided for every ten pounds I lost, I would get a new outfit. The first time I went shopping I realized I didn't know what I wanted to look like so I didn't know what to buy. I went home in tears. Twelve weeks after Hal left I bought a new lavender suit with a skirt, blouse, jacket and slacks, size 12— the smallest I had worn in fifteen years. I felt so proud of myself.

"I had made two new friends at the fitness center, so we went out to celebrate with a game of tennis. After the match one of the women asked me if I would like to volunteer to raise money for the children's museum. I didn't want to but I said I'd be glad to. I knew I needed to push myself or I would be in the same old rut.

"I made myself do one thing a day for myself. Call a friend, read an article, polish my nails, play tennis, listen to music. I found I loved jazz.

"After six months I had lost twenty-one pounds and I felt great as I took my lavender suit in to be altered. I had a life. I started to care about my home, too. It was a mess. I sorted through old clothes, dinnerware, old toys and furniture we didn't want and got rid of twenty-two boxes of stuff. I made $585 at our garage sale. I painted the living room and bought some new prints for the walls. I scrubbed the bathrooms, painted, got new towels and made matching shower curtains from sheets. A friend helped me wallpaper the bedroom and I bought new lavender sheets and made a dark purple duvet cover and pillow shams trimmed in lavender and green. I put sprays of baby's breath and bowls of potpourri in the bedroom and bathroom. It looks and smells the way I feel, pretty, inviting and sensual. The whole project cost less than the money from the sale.

"I think what felt so good was I was doing things myself, making my own choices and finding out I had good taste and good judgment. Friends started asking me to make duvet covers, pillow shams and shower curtains for them.

"It has been a year since Hal left. I have a nice sewing business. I make a good income, enough to not have to ask Hal for extra money. I have terrific friends, a great social life, and I contribute to our community by working at the food bank. I exercise every day and I am dating a great guy. He likes jazz, tennis and exercise, and most of all he loves lavender. His name is Hal."

When Hal left, Liz thought her life was over. In truth it was just beginning. She took responsibility for herself and for meeting her needs. She learned to feel her emotions and she learned to think about who she wanted to be and how she wanted her life to work. Liz took control of her life and empowered herself to be a creative, fully alive woman.

▼ Summary

An affair does not necessarily mean a marriage is bad. However, affairs do threaten the bonds of trust, honesty and integrity that are essential to a healthy marriage.

Discovery of an affair is a traumatic shock with both physical and emotional consequences. View this time in your life as abnormal and make extra effort to care for and protect yourself. Go beyond your usual routine to focus on your physical and emotional health. Give yourself extra time for exercise, meditation and good nutrition. Stay close to the people who care about you.

Depression is common during times like this. If you are feeling emotionally flat, unsteady and lifeless, talk to a physician or counselor about the options for treating depression. Don't just accept depression as normal. It is not! This is a dangerous time in your life. *Please, take good care of yourself.*

Learn new skills that will help you cope with this crisis and will also help resolve current and future problems. Learn to express your feelings, but also think. Don't be in a hurry to resolve the problems brought to light by the affair. Hurrying the solutions will not shorten the pain.

PART 5

Advice for the Couple: Affair-Proof Your Marriage

Today's divorce rate for recent, first time marriages is 67%. Sadly, the divorce rate for remarriages is over 75%. Affairs are a factor in 25% to 50% of these divorces. An affair is a realistic threat to any marriage. For those who want a lifetime marriage, actively protecting and maintaining your marriage is essential.

▼ IS YOUR MARRIAGE AFFAIR-PROOF?

1. Do you save prime time and prime energy for your partner?
2. Do you schedule time to fight?
3. Do you commit to a regular time to make love?
4. Do you compliment one another at least five times a day?
5. Do you smile and kiss your spouse hello and good-bye?

6. Do you talk about your spouse as though you are proud of him or her?
7. Do you intentionally think about how you talk to and listen to your partner so you can understand them rather than making them understand you?

These questions address important behaviors in creating an affair-proof marriage by being each other's lover. Whenever I suggest to couples that they schedule time to make love and time to fight, I hear groans and objections. The typical reaction: "planning time for sex is boring," or "planning time to fight is silly, fights just happen". While there is certainly some merit to these reactions, there is just not enough time and energy left over in our busy lives to spontaneously meet our intimacy needs. Making love regularly and resolving conflicts expediently are crucial to keeping a marriage safe. An affair-proof marriage takes thinking, feeling, communicating and actively choosing to be each other's friend, partner and lover day to day.

There are three elements which have to be present in the foundation of your marriage before you can create a secure marriage.

▶ A commitment to know and meet each others needs

▶ The discipline to know and to live your values and to support your spouse's values

▶ Acceptance of responsibility for your own happiness and a willingness to contribute generously to your spouse's happiness

Before a marriage can be affair-proof it has to have a solid foundation and be basically healthy and happy.

▲
▲
▲
▲
▲
▲
▲
▲
▲
▲

16

What Is an Affair-Proof Marriage?

I have been counseling people during the past two decades to create happy, healthy lifetime marriages. Here is a summation of what my clients report is important in their marriages:

1. Best friends—I want to know we are best friends, that we look out for each other, confide in one another and would never betray each other.
2. Loving—I want to hear and to say I love you every day and mean it.
3. Romantic—I want a marriage in which we communicate the love we feel in a multitude of ways: talking, touching, writing and just fooling around.
4. Sexually fulfilling—I want a relationship that is actively sexual and sensual where sex can be close, intimate and serious and it can be fun, silly or naughty.
5. Supportive—It is important to me to feel safe, secure and stable so we can try new things and grow in new areas both separately and together.

A loving, romantic, sexy, supportive marriage to your best friend doesn't just happen by chance!

One or two of these qualities are not enough; it takes all of them to have a successful lifetime marriage. An affair-proof marriage takes a lot of work, requiring thought, skill, discipline and determination.

The basis for a lasting and happy marriage is a commitment to know and meet each other's needs. While we all have the same needs, the way we get our needs met is not the same. Often, we mistakenly give what we would like to receive rather than giving what our partner needs. Learn how to give and receive to meet each other's needs.

Read the emotional needs listed below, then make your list adding others you have identified. Rank them in the order of importance they have to you. Underline the needs which are being met. (Remember, met needs are easily overlooked.) Next put a check mark by three of the needs which you would like to focus on now.

- ▸ Giving love
- ▸ Receiving love
- ▸ Respect and appreciation
- ▸ Caring for others
- ▸ Being needed
- ▸ Feeling understood and accepted
- ▸ Excitement and enjoyable risk
- ▸ Challenge or adventure
- ▸ Freedom and independence
- ▸ Friendship
- ▸ Fun

▶ Intellectual stimulation
▶ Sexual fulfillment
▶ Recognition of contributions

List the behaviors which meet your emotional needs. Add other behaviors that work for you. Complete the lists separately, then discuss them with one another. Identify other ways of meeting each other's needs.

▶ Intimate conversation
▶ Positive compliments
▶ Touching
▶ Eye contact
▶ Public expression of appreciation
▶ Pillow talk
▶ Sex
▶ Affection
▶ Making love
▶ Playing together
▶ Sharing new experiences
▶ Humor
▶ Working
▶ Learning together
▶ Helping

Jamie and Wally committed to learning about each other's emotional needs so they could have a strong, intimate relationship that would help them avoid another painful affair.

Wally recalls, "Twenty-five years of marriage and Jamie

and I are still in love. Not the giddy kind of love but a deep love and appreciation of one another. We had an affair crisis about twelve years ago but we got through it. I learned that Jamie was truly my best friend. She didn't try to punish me or embarrass me. She stepped up to the plate and said, 'We have to learn to be better at meeting each other's needs because I want you to be my life's partner.' That was what I wanted too—a lifetime partner."

Wally and Jamie took time to examine and communicate their emotional needs. As Jamie says, "After we made our lists, we started talking about what we meant to each other. What our ideal relationship would be (the same way lovers do). I wanted to love and be loved more than anything else and he wanted to be understood and respected. I was surprised. I thought he just wanted more sex. He said, 'I probably would want more sex if I felt like you were interested in me, liked me and respected me.' I was dumbfounded. How could he think I didn't like, respect or appreciate him?

"I looked at the behaviors he had circled—positive compliments, public appreciation and affection. I assumed I knew what he wanted. I realized I criticized what I didn't like and didn't say much about the things I thought were fine. Not anymore. I look for all the qualities I like in Wally and tell him. It is fun. The more I look, the more I find. I tell my friends and our families about his wonderful qualities and all the nice things he does and I make it a point to touch him. These simple things dramatically changed our marriage."

According to Wally, "I knew Jamie wanted to feel loved, and I loved her, but when I looked at the behaviors that signaled my love to her I could see why she didn't feel my love. She needs me to look into her eyes, touch her, hold her and whisper loving feelings to her especially at bedtime. Now it seems so obvious and so easy."

Psychological needs are the motivation for many love affairs. Be aware of your own needs and your spouse's needs all the time. Needs are in a constant state of flux; one of the joys and complexities of being human is our ever-changing needs. Set a time each year to review and update your list. Also, think daily about how your lover gives and receives love then give all you can.

The goal of a healthy marriage is to meet each other's needs as they arise, not to dole out our resources as we think they should be needed. The same attitudes and behaviors that make a marriage fulfilling prevent affairs. Make a commitment to know and meet each other's needs.

▼ VALUES AND CHOICES

A solid marriage requires the discipline to know and to live your values, and to support your spouse's values. The more consistency between lifestyle, behavior and values, the greater the sense of satisfaction a person will feel. It is easy to drift away from living our values because of the pace of modern life and the complexity of society's demands.

Identifying values gives a marriage definition and direction. The blending of individual values adds strength to a marriage and allows a couple to achieve their goals and attain a better quality of life. It is important to take an inventory of personal values to see if they are consistent with choices you are making daily. A list of values and ways of behaving follows. Add to these lists, drawing from your own thoughts. Think about your values and how they are reflected in your behavior.

Common Values
Identify your three most important values and write them on a piece of paper. Expand the lists below to personalize it if you wish.

Financial success
Altruism
Equality
Loving relationships
Independence
Inner peace
Intimacy
Power
Spirituality
Positive self-esteem
Friendship
Recognition
Personal growth
An exciting life
Sensual and sexual pleasure

Behavior
Identify your three most important behaviors. Write them on the same paper; compare the two lists. Do your most important ways of behaving lead you to your most important values?

Hard-working
Disciplined
Accepting
Patient
Helpful to others
Honest

Creative
Playful
Sexy
Sensual

Find Common Ground

One purpose of a healthy marriage is to support each other's values and to achieve life goals. Compare your list of values and behavior with your spouse's list. Talk about every one of the items on your list to know what they mean to each of you. Treat this as a learning experience, not a competition. No one is right or wrong.

Talk to one another about how your behaviors help you to live your values or how they interfere. Create a combined list which includes both sets of values. Next to each of the values, list your behaviors which help you to live your values.

Graham is a chief operating officer for a software company. He is a gourmet cook and an athlete. He runs twenty miles a week, plays basketball and enjoys household carpentry.

Arlene is an designer for an architectural firm. She is a people person with dozens of good friends. She is usually involved helping friends decorate and furnish their homes. Graham and Arlene's home is a show piece inside and out with an ever-changing decor and beautiful outdoor gardens.

Arlene and Graham were shaken when their best friends divorced during an affair. Their friends explained, "We just don't have anything in common anymore. We grew apart." Arlene and Graham decided they wanted to be sure they didn't end up in the same situation. They each made a list of their top three values and behaviors.

Arlene's Values

Loving Relationships
Intimacy
Personal Growth

Arlene's Behaviors

Helpful to others
Hardworking
Creative

Graham's Values

Financial success
Sensual and sexual pleasure
Intimacy

Graham's Behaviors

Hardworking
Healthy eating and activity
Disciplined

Both Graham and Arlene were surprised that their behaviors were definitely not taking them toward their goals. While hard work would probably get Graham financial success, his enjoyment of eating and carpentry were not going to create sexual pleasure or intimacy.

It became clear to Arlene that helping others gave her more loving relationships and her creativity aided her personal growth, but the emphasis she placed on working hard at her job, in her home and in her yard were not putting her on a path to intimacy with Graham.

Arlene says, "We were very busy with dinner guests

because of my desire to have close relationships and Graham's love of food, we entertained several times a week. It dawned on us that we were spending nearly all our best time and energy entertaining others or doing household projects."

Graham and Arlene created a plan to make their most important values fit more closely with their behaviors. One of their first changes was their social schedule. Graham explains, "We decided since this is our primary relationship we should be spending 'prime time.' Saturday night is our weekend date night. We plan something special. We still get together with friends but our first priority is each other. Now we check with each other before we make separate plans including additional work hours."

Live Your Values and Support Your Spouse's Values

1. Your goal as a couple is to support one another in finding ways to incorporate your primary values into your day-to-day life.

2. Compare your list of values and behavior with your spouse's list. They will not all be the same.

3. Ask clarifying questions of one another. Values can be interpreted differently.

4. Help one another to identify behaviors that support values or undermine them.

5. Do not criticize, blame or condemn each other's choices.

6. Talk to one another as you would talk to a close friend.

Reviewing your values and behaviors on an annual basis keeps you on track. It is very easy to react to opportunities and drift away from what is really important to you. Happy people actively live their values.

▼ HAPPY PEOPLE—HAPPY MARRIAGES

"Remember that the 'big bang' achievements are not as important, in terms of life satisfaction, as the sum total of all the little moments. Being able to recognize everyday pleasures is every bit as vital as achieving new ones."

—ALEX C. MICHALOS, PH.D., *PSYCHOLOGY TODAY*,
JULY/AUGUST 1994

People who are happy with themselves are the most likely to be happy in their marriages, rather than the other way around. Although it is not possible to make someone else happy, it is important to instigate and embrace everyday pleasures.

Major positive events are memorable and can enhance a happy marriage, but it is the little things that often count the most. My cousin, Marcia, reminded me of our granddad's wisdom in a story he told of one of his life's love lessons. He recalled, "I was going out to mow the lawn and your grandma asked me to mow around a small little patch of wild flowers that had appeared after the winter thaw. I nodded. When I started mowing and looked at those little flowers, I thought, 'They are nothing special and it will take extra time to mow around them.' So, on the next round I mowed over them. When I turned around I looked up and saw your grandmother looking out the window with tears in her eyes. She said nothing, but I realized I had been a fool. Mowing around those flowers would have been such a little thing and so easy to do— a simple thing I could do for my wife."

I have thought of my granddad's words many times as I have listened to couples stubbornly refuse to grant one another small favors. So often these small gestures are minor inconveniences at the most and they mean so much. Make an unexpected phone call, leave a light on if your spouse is out after dark, play her favorite song, watch his favorite program together, bring home a treat. Do something just to bring a smile to his face.

Simple pleasures are the sources of our best memories. They are the simple things that make us smile when we recall them, and they are usually free.

▼
A Few Simple Pleasures
▸ Walking hand-in-hand
▸ Singing together
▸ Sharing a milkshake
▸ Reading the comics together
▸ Cuddling in front of the fire

If someone is chronically unhappy, no marriage will transform him into a happy person. Although marriages do not in themselves make people happy, healthy marriages do offer good interpersonal relationships and enhance self esteem. They can provide the opportunity and encouragement for new experiences, learning and challenges. Medical studies show that both men and women who are happy in their marriage live longer with better health. Happy marriages contribute to our physical and mental health, sense of well-being and productivity.

What Makes People Happy

1. Good interpersonal relationships with friends and family
2. Positive self-esteem
3. Good physical health
4. Knowing we have control over our lives
5. Absorption in meaningful activity
6. Having new experiences and new learning

Psychology Today, 1994

Accept responsibility for your own happiness and be willing to contribute generously to your spouse's happiness—daily! Happiness comes, in part, from the day-to-day savoring of simple pleasures. Simple pleasures are the source of our best memories. They are the silly things that make us smile when we recall them. Create magic in your marriage by finding something special to do for one another every day.

▼ SUMMARY

Be committed to knowing and meeting each other's needs. Stay current with your own and your partner's values and accept responsibility for your own happiness. Be willing to contribute generously to your spouse's happiness and you will have a good foundation for a lifetime marriage.

Knowing and meeting each other's needs is a major factor in creating a solid foundation for a marriage. Change is constant. Every day we have different experiences, new lessons and fresh feelings. The opportunity to learn and know one another anew is always present.

Anthony was entranced by his new secretary, Eva. She made him feel young and alive again. Margy, his wife of twenty-five years, made him feel old; she was boring and set in her ways. It wasn't until his affair with Eva was discovered that he and Margy really opened up.

Anthony says, "Margy was so predictable. I was bored. She was like an old shoe. She was just there. We had our routine. I came home tired, she made dinner, we watched TV or went out to a movie. We seldom talked. I was unhappy in our marriage.

"Thinking we would separate, we started listening to each other and talking more about our mistakes, our feelings, our disappointments, our fun times, our mutual sense of humor and the love we used to share."

Margy explained, "You are like an emotional desert. You are flat, cold and isolated. You were unwilling to try anything new. I couldn't find your heart. Basically, I have been lonely so I found a friend."

"Margy told me things about herself I never would have believed. Margy had an affair five years earlier. With her lover, she had learned to scuba dive and wind surf. She had even sky-dived.

"That was ten years ago. It was the beginning of our new marriage. I was so shocked by what I found out I wanted to know more. I realized my unhappiness wasn't because of Margy. She wasn't the one who was boring. I was bored and unhappy with myself and my life.

"I had pretty much withdrawn from everything but work. I focused on making money, putting together deals and treating myself to expensive meals. I guess it's no wonder I got involved with my secretary. If someone wasn't interested in my work, I wasn't interested in her. During this crisis, I started thinking about my values, about what used to be important to me. Boy, was I off track. I had to do some serious soul search-ing.

"Now, Margy and I treat each other like the most impor-tant person in our world. We spend hours every week talking about what we are doing, what we are thinking, about our needs, our values, our hopes and our dreams.

"We take turns planning something special weekly as well as every other weekend. My world has grown and so have I. Now we have a sailboat and we race once a week, we go together to work for the community services for the elderly, we go to the theater, we even go to rock concerts.

"And then there is sex, rather making love. What a differ-ence from ten years ago. Now, we have so much fun being lovers. She always liked little presents, so I started getting lit-tle things she would like and hiding them. I started talking to her more about how beautiful she is to look at, inside and out. I ask her to do little experiments with me, I try to discover what might bring a smile to her face or laughter to her lips. It is like a treasure hunt. I'm always looking for little clues about what would be precious to Margy."

Anthony found he could make his marriage better than an affair by learning about himself and Margy. He brought his marriage back to life when he shook off his prejudice and rediscovered himself and his wife.

Make your marriage the best it can be—by being the best you can be. Offer your emotional resources to one another generously—not sparingly—and without judgment or condi-tions. Continually look at your mate to discover and rediscover all that is there. Don't assume you know what the other needs. Investigate, then meet those needs, eagerly and enthu-siastically!

If you aren't happy, look to yourself first. Are you doing all you can to be connected to each other emotionally, to improve your self-esteem, to make good choices for your physical and mental health and to be absorbed in meaningful activities and have new experiences?

If you have a marriage founded on a willingness to be committed to knowing and meeting each other's needs, if you are living your values and if you are basically happy with yourself and are willing to contribute generously to your spouse's happiness, you have a very good chance of developing a lifetime, affair-proof marriage. Success in creating a lasting marriage starts with excellent communication.

▶ 17

Strengthening Communication

A marriage can only be as good as the communication.

"I am listening. I can repeat everything you said," or "Yeah, yeah, I know,"—if either of these phrases is a familiar part of your conversation, you have a communication problem. Communication is sending, giving or exchanging information. As trite as it sounds, communication is the biggest problem in most marriages and it holds the best solutions.

There are three types of communication that improve intimacy and understanding. They are active listening, investigative exploration and intimate communication.

Active listening may be the most important single skill you can use. It is the basis for all types of intimate communication.

Active listening is a simple tool which is tedious at times, but it works. There are two different roles in active listening, the role of the sender and the role of the receiver. When sending communication, speak simply and briefly, then give the receiver a chance to paraphrase what they have heard.

As the listener, listen carefully and attentively. Repeat what you hear in your own words. Wait until you both agree that the message sent is the message received before going on to the next point. Be slow and thorough.

Focus is a key element in active listening. Lola and Jonathan nearly split up because Lola thought Jonathan didn't respect or understand her. When Lola told Jonathan she wanted a divorce, he was mystified. Finally, she told him about her affair, but she insisted that the affair was not the reason she wanted a divorce. She told him, "The affair is over and I have no future with Keith, but I learned from Keith what is missing in our marriage. When I was with Keith, he listened to me and wanted me to talk to him. He asked me questions, and he paid attention to what I said."

Jonathan argued, "I want you to talk to me, and I think I'm a good listener." Lola responded angrily, "No, you aren't, Jonathan. I'm tired of saying the same thing over and over. You always say, 'Yes, I hear you,' and you can repeat exactly what I said, verbatim. It just all seems empty to me. You act like what I have to say is stupid, and you brush me off."

Lola is describing a classic example of inactive listening. Jonathan can repeat what she has said but clearly doesn't understand the emotional component of the message being sent. The sender, Lola, feels frustration and disrespect.

Jonathan was astonished to find that it was his unfocused listening that Lola so deeply resented. When she confessed her affair, he listened and learned.

Jonathan's willingness to learn active listening skills was essential before they could improve their marriage. Jonathan now says, "I thought I was a good communicator. I didn't know what I was missing. Listening is a lot more than hearing what someone says."

Whether couples are loud or quiet in their communication does not matter, but interactive communication of thoughts and feelings that show respect is essential to marital health.

Feeling heard and understood is part of feeling loved, so remember:

▶ Receiver—focus with your undivided attention and make eye contact with your partner while you listen.

▶ Sender—speak briefly, then wait for a response and stick to one point per exchange.

▶ Both—actively listen, be friendly and courteous and take turns sending and receiving.

▼ Don and Alicia's Communication

Old Style

Alicia: "I'm tired."

Don: "Me, too."

Alicia: "What do you want for dinner?"

Don: "Hmm, how about some pasta and maybe a salad?"

Alicia: "OK. What are you doing?"

Don: "Turning on the game."

Alicia spent the evening noisily making dinner. Don thought she was mad because he wanted to watch the game. He felt resentful, and she went to bed angry.

NEW STYLE: ACTIVE LISTENING

Alicia: "I'm tired."

Don: "You're tired?"

Alicia: "Yeah. What do you want for dinner?"

Don: "You want to know what I want for dinner and you're tired?"

Alicia: "I'm tired, but I'll fix something."

Don: "You want to fix dinner?"

Alicia: "No, I don't want to, but I will."

Don: "You don't want to fix dinner, but you will?"

Alicia: "Sure, if it's important to you."

Don: "You'll fix dinner, if it's important to me?"

Alicia: "Yes, if you want me to."

Don: "I don't want you to make dinner. I'll fix a sandwich and watch baseball if you want to do something else."

Alicia: "Great, I think I'll just go to bed early."

In their former communication style, Don would have heard that Alicia was tired, then he would have shifted his focus. By repeating her words back to her, he got additional information. She clarified that being tired was only part of the message. The most significant part of the communication—that Alicia did not want to fix dinner—was originally not stated. Thanks to Don's active listening, they didn't have a dinner neither wanted, and both had a good evening.

▼ INVESTIGATIVE EXPLORATION

Investigative exploration is an essential tool in developing emotional intimacy. Investigative exploration means seeking and examining information in a style that is curious and non-judgmental. The purpose is to inquire about one another to gain deeper understanding and knowledge. Learning about one another leads to intimacy.

Investigative communication takes active listening skills, plus the desire to learn more about each other emotionally. Listen carefully, paraphrase and be very sure there is a clear understanding of what both you and your spouse are and are not saying. Investigative communication helps develop strong emotional bonds.

Be careful—full of care—about what you say, how you say it and when you say it so you don't arouse defenses. If your partner becomes defensive—wait. There is no hurry, you have plenty of time to learn about each other by being persistent and interested.

Alicia found that investigative exploration gave her a much deeper understanding of Don, and she was surprised at what she discovered.

OLD STYLE

Alicia: "Let's go to a movie."

Don: "Sure, if you want to."

Alicia: "What do you want to see?"

Don: "I don't care."

Alicia: "Don, you complained last week that we didn't do anything fun, now you act like I'm dragging you out."

Don: "Alicia, a movie is fine, if that is what you want."

Alicia: "We have not been out on a date for two weeks. Why don't you ever want to do anything with me?"

Don: "Forget it, Alicia, a movie is fine."

Alicia: "You are such a drag, you spoil the fun."

NEW STYLE: INVESTIGATIVE EXPLORATION

Alicia: "Let's go to a movie."

Don: "Sure, if you want to."

Alicia: "What do you want to see?"

Don: "I don't care."

Alicia: "You don't care, or you don't want to go to a movie?"

Don: "Movies are OK, but they're not my idea of a great date."

ALICIA BEGINS INVESTIGATIVE EXPLORATION

Alicia: "Movies aren't your idea of a great date. Do you want a great date?"

Don: "Yeah, I would like a great date. Our last great date was a long time ago."

Alicia: "You would like a great date, but we haven't had one in a long time. Don, are you disappointed we haven't had enough time together, enough fun or enough sex?"

Don: "It seems like we haven't had fun by ourselves for a long time, and I miss the times we used to have."

Alicia: "What comes to mind when you think of the fun we used to have?"

Don: "Remember when we used to go play pool and then walk down to Pluto's Bar and dance? Sometimes we went to Sam's for a midnight breakfast."

Alicia: "I remember that, and I do miss our fun times."

Don: "I don't find movies that much fun. We don't talk, and a week later I hardly remember what we saw. I miss the time we used to spend together. I never thought I would be the one complaining about not enough talking, but I miss our talks. Tonight I would rather have a glass of wine in the living room and just talk to you."

Alicia was astonished and delighted to discover that Don missed talking to her and wanted to have a simple evening alone with her. She often felt burdened figuring out their social plans and choose going to a movie because she thought she knew he liked movies. Through investigative exploration she learned something knew about her husband. It is easy to rely on old information assuming that we know each other. Stay current with your partner—everyone changes.

▼ INTIMATE COMMUNICATION

Intimate communication is revealing and bonding. It brings us closest to discovering our natural selves.

Intimate communication is the sharing of your deepest nature. Intimate communication fully engulfs both partners and leads to learning about the inner self. Intimate communication requires skill, focus, trust, patience and quiet.

You must feel safe, close and loved before you can be vulnerable enough to explore and share your innermost self.

Create an environment that is intimate. Choose a place that is warm, quiet and nurturing. Only communicate intimately when you both feel good about yourselves and each other.

1. Schedule an hour for intimate communication once a month.
2. Sit in a position where you can see your spouse. Look into each other's eyes.
3. Hold each other's hands while you listen and speak with your ears, your eyes, your mouth and your heart. Communicate with your whole being.
4. Be gentle, kind and tender with each other.

DON AND ALICIA'S INTIMATE COMMUNICATION

Don: "I feel calm and relaxed when you touch me. It reminds me of our trip to Hawaii."

Alicia: "When I touch you it reminds you of Hawaii?"

Don: "No, not just of Hawaii. Your caressing my neck gives me the same feeling I felt in Hawaii. I feel close, connected and tender. Sometimes when I feel this way it scares me."

Alicia: "Your feelings scare you?"

Don: "Yes, when I realize how much you mean to me and I cannot imagine life without you. Sometimes I think I should pull back and be more independent."

Alicia: "Do you want to be more independent?"

Don: "No, being so closely connected to you is the best feeling I have ever had. I just get scared when I think someday one of us will be without the other."

Alicia: "I feel a chill when I think of being without you. It makes me want to make every minute count. I want you to feel the love I have in my heart."

Don: "I feel your love when I hold you and feel your heart beating next to mine, I hear nothing but the sound of your breathing and smell only the scent of your hair."

Intimate communication is an extraordinary experience. It is difficult to sustain vulnerability and emotional clarity for very long. It takes practice and patience. I think it is the best feeling you can ever have with the one you love.

10 Principles for Loving Communication

1. Encourage communication.
2. Listen to the thoughts.
3. Listen to the feelings.
4. Send messages that convey both thoughts and feelings.
5. Believe what you hear.
6. Respond to what you hear, not to what you think is right.
7. Remember—most people want to feel understood and accepted, positively.
8. Express your feelings using feeling words.

9. Identify thoughts as thoughts.

10. Wait until the listener understands before you move on to other feelings or thoughts..

▼ FREQUENT COMPLAINTS

My partner is:

▶ Hearing, but not listening.

▶ Listening, but not believing.

▶ Believing, but not caring.

Communication takes skill. It probably determines more about a marriage than any other single component. Learn, practice and continually develop loving communication skills.

▼ NEGOTIATION

We all have differences. Differences can create tension; they also create an opportunity to learn, experience and grow. Intimacy is based on learning, understanding and acceptance. Intimacy is developed through negotiation.

Getting Together, Building Relationships As We Negotiate, written by Roger Fisher and Scott Brown of the Harvard Negotiation Project, offers clear directions on negotiating. Intimate negotiations should be based on the idea that both parties are positive, constructive and honorable. Healthy partners "win" through understanding and accepting each other. The agreements reached through negotiation must work for the benefit of the couple. If one of the spouses loses, both ultimately lose. Win/win solutions are the only good outcomes in intimate relationships.

▼

Guidelines for Negotiating in an Intimate Relationship

1. Designate a time and a place to negotiate.
2. Plan what you want to talk about ahead of time.
3. Distinguish between feelings, thoughts and issues.
4. Listen to feelings with empathy.
5. Wait until you are both finished expressing feelings before you offer solutions.
6. Carefully and clearly identify the issues, options and solutions.
7. Do not start on another topic until the first one is either resolved or tabled.
8. Offer suggestions about the issue, not each other.
9. Never criticize each other.
10. Be affirming, constructive and honorable.

Clark and Corry attribute their marital success to being top notch negotiators. Corry and Clark have the same conflicts other couples do, but they look forward to talking through their disagreements.

Corry usually schedules a negotiating session when they know they have a disagreement. They plan on an hour Saturday or Sunday morning when neither is tired. Clark says, "Our last meeting was about how we were spending our time. We take turns running the meeting. This time it was my turn."

Clark: "I see the problem as poor scheduling of our time."

Corry: "Well, I don't. I see the problem as having too much going on. I feel ragged by the weekend. I'm frustrated because I'm always behind. The weekend comes and I spend time catching up just to start again on Monday."

Clark: "It sounds like you feel overwhelmed by all you have to do as opposed to organizing our schedule better."

Corry: "Yes. I think we need to prioritize better. I just cannot do everything I'm committed to."

Clark: "OK, let's make a list of all the things you are doing, then go through and mark them as one, two or three in importance."

By the end of their first hour of negotiating Clark and Corry had a list. They chose to eliminate every item that was rated as a three on Corry's list by either delegating it to someone else or dropping it from her list. They agreed to meet the following Saturday and talk about what had and had not worked. Both agreed to think about how they were spending their time and what they could give up.

After their session Corry said, "I think the reason I like to negotiate with Clark is because we help each other figure out what is going on and we are a resource for each other." Clark and Corry were able to define the problem without blaming or criticizing one another. There was no blame or defensiveness. They talked like friends trying to find a solution to a mutual problem.

▼ MARITAL HAPPINESS COMES FROM BEING TRUE TO YOURSELF AND EACH OTHER

1. Consider your values.
2. Decide if they are expressed in your life.
3. Evaluate who you have become.
4. Ask—are you the best you can be?
5. Decide on the changes you will make.
6. Make changes to be the person you want to be.
7. Be complimentary with yourself and others.
8. Live your values day to day.
9. Identify and savor your little successes.

Arlene and Graham and Corry and Clark say the most important lesson in changing their marriages was learning several ways to communicate. They found that effective communication is as simple as active listening. If they are negotiating, they have use investigative exploration, and if they want to be emotionally close, they use intimate communication skills. The communication skills they learned have become one of their most valued tools in creating the marriages they want.

18

Affair-Proof Your Marriage: Be Each Other's Lover

▼ **AFFAIR-PROOF YOUR MARRIAGE—BE PROTECTIVE, POSITIVE, POLITE, PLAYFUL AND HAVE A PLAN!**

The key to affair-proofing your marriage is to be each other's lover. That means being protective, positive, polite and playful. Success in creating an affair-proof marriage requires planning and scheduling. Marriages are created. They are developed by the daily choices we make. Whether we choose to make each other a top priority or to put our jobs, kids, exercise, friends or sports ahead of our mate determines how affair-proof a marriage is. Lovers make each other a priority. If you want to be each other's lover, then you have to live it on a day-to-day basis.

Numerous men and women have confided that they would never have believed that they nor their spouse would ever have had an affair. An affair can happen in any marriage. It is the everyday texture of the relationship that ultimately determines its strength or frailty.

The best ways I have found to affair proof a marriage are:

1. Be *protective* of your marriage. Avoid risky situations like long lunches with a coworker or drinks for two after work. Most people do not plan to be unfaithful.

2. Be *positive*. Look for what is right in your spouse and tell them daily. People who have love affairs are often looking for appreciation, respect and understanding.

3. Be *polite*. Always talk to your spouse with respect. Be careful what you say to each other and how you say it. Show courtesy and caring in the way you treat one another.

4. Be *playful*. Make fun, sex and humor a mainstay of your marriage. Schedule time to play with one another and have a date night at least once a week.

5. Be a *planner*. Schedule time to create and maintain the type of marriage you want, including time to be each other's lover.

▼ BE PROTECTIVE OF YOUR MARRIAGE

A major factor in affairs is opportunity. Those who have control over their time are the most likely to take a lover. Sooner or later, exposure to a member of the opposite sex results in a physiological or psychological attraction. PEA can be increased in anyone, overriding their good intentions. Physiological and psychological needs drive behavior, and those who have the time and energy to pursue their desires—often do! Stay out of situations that pose a threat to your marriage. Hazards are warning signs. Watch for them.

Hazards
- ▸ Not sleeping together
- ▸ Spending more than four evenings a week apart
- ▸ Lengthy lunches for two with a coworker
- ▸ Quiet drinks after work with a coworker
- ▸ Separate vacations

Jerinne and Adam felt secure in their marriage and thought of themselves as independent people. Jerinne began to feel jealous while Adam was telling her a joke Marline had told him. At first, she brushed off her feeling and was irritated with herself for being jealous.

As she began talking about her feelings, she recognized her recurrent jealousy as a warning signal and thought maybe her marriage was at risk for an affair. She and Adam talked about the fact that he did often have lunch with Marline and that their conversations were becoming more personal.

Adam and Jerinne had stopped sleeping together because his loud snoring woke her up during the night. They acknowledged that since they had stopped sleeping together they didn't make love as often. Jerinne was an avid skier, and while Adam liked skiing, he had a knee injury that interfered, so she went skiing with a friend. Adam said he didn't mind since he could catch up on work. Adam often worked late into the evening so Jerinne met friends after work for a drink or dinner. Jerinne and Adam's lives were becoming increasingly separate.

Adam and Jerinne had a fight after Adam commented that he looked forward to seeing Marline every day. He joked, "I spend more time with Marline that I do with my wife." Adam and Jerinne decided they were exposing their marriage to more hazards than seemed wise.

My advice to Jerinne and Adam:

▸ Sleep together. Sleeping next to each other develops intimate unconscious bonds of trust and connection through touching, cuddling and falling asleep together. Snoring is commonly a physical problem, so talk to your doctor about medical options. My clients have found ear plugs that work, white noise devices that even out the sounds and special pillows designed to improve breathing.

▸ Two to three nights a week of going out without each other is enough to give a couple independence. Some evening events are healthy and necessary. Make them early evenings with opposite-sex friends. After eight—it's a date.

▸ Keep work at work. Long lunches for two or drinks after work with a coworker are a setup for intimacy. The highest percentage of women's affairs are with coworkers. It doesn't take long to relax and for the conversation to become more personal, more fun and more intimate.

It is easy and dangerous to become comfortable in your marriage and to think of these hazards as little problems everyone has. Big mistake. If you see these hazards in your marriage, address them now and come up with solutions that lower the risk of an affair. Protect your marriage.

▼ BE POSITIVE

Catch your partner doing something right and say so. Pay attention to the little things. We tend to find what we are looking for. If we look for mistakes, we find them. If we look for disappointments, they are all around us. On the other hand when we look for kindness, we see it, and when we look for love, encouragement or support, we find it, too.

Hazards
- ▶ Belittling comments
- ▶ Hostile humor (put-downs with a laugh)
- ▶ Criticism
- ▶ Taking each other for granted

Betsy and Jay came to counseling after a big blowup when Jay came home very late for the third time. As we talked, Betsy joked, "It's not that I really want him home. He drives me nuts (*ha-ha*)." Later she remarked, "With his luck, if he did try to pick someone up she would probably take his money and run (*chuckle, chuckle*)." He responded, "I don't have to worry about anyone picking you up, Butts!" Jay looked at me and added, "Butts is my nickname for her since she gained ten, fifteen and twenty pounds." When I asked them if this was their normal repartee, they both nodded enthusiastically and quickly added, "We're just kidding each other."

When I asked them to look each other in the eye, hold hands and say the same thing without laughing, Jay and Betsy resisted. When Jay repeated his words, Betsy started to cry.

Betsy then launched into a tirade about all the things Jay

didn't do and exclaimed, "I'm tired of nagging." Jay chuckled, replying, "Why bother? Anything I do, you do over."

My advice to Jay and Betsy was that they were damaging their marriage by being careless rather than careful. Their humor was hurtful, not funny, and they were not being effective at getting what they needed from one another. I suggested:

▶ Compliment each other and catch your partner doing something right and say so at least five times a day (count).

▶ Use forethought. Think about what you like and respect in your partner—attitudes, skills and talents, for instance.

▶ Be generous and enthusiastic in recognizing all the good qualities in your mate.

▶ Adopt an attitude of goodwill and good humor.

▶ Stop all criticism and advice giving. It is fine to complain but never to criticize.

▶ If you're joking around, look at your partner eye to eye, take their hands and say the same thing without laughing—is it loving or hurtful?

On a daily basis, take a minute to look into your spouse's eyes, remember that this is your mate, the person you love, and say something loving. There is plenty of research to prove that criticism destroys intimacy. Deliver, in a loving tone, those five compliments a day. Count to be sure. Think ahead about qualities, characteristics and behaviors you like, respect and appreciate and make a decision to compliment your partner. While I brush my teeth, I routinely think about my husband's generosity, his sense of humor and his good deeds. It's a great way to begin and end the day.

Don't wait for perfection—it doesn't exist! Don't correct

your partner when he is doing something for you. Assume he has good intentions. While he may not do things the way you would, it is probably good enough, and good enough is good. Simply smile and say thank you.

We are good at remembering the bad. Think about whether it is really important before you point out wrongs. There is wisdom in the adage "If you can't say something good, don't say anything at all."

If you have an issue, wait and think it over. If it is important, schedule a time when you can be alone and uninterrupted to talk it over and find a solution. If you are fighting about the same issue over and over, schedule a series of meetings to solve the problem (see Chapter 17). If you are not able to come to a resolution, get help. Nothing destroys a relationship faster than unresolved issues that turn into criticism.

Be positive with your partner and create a marriage you are proud of.

▼ BE POLITE

Good manners are a sign of respect. Courtesy and respect create strong bonds between people, and spouses are no exception. The tone many couples use when talking to one another is not one they would use with anyone else and certainly not with their friends.

Hazards
▶ Not stopping to look and listen when your partner is talking
▶ Rolling eyes, exasperated sighs, talking over the other person
▶ Giving orders rather than making requests

A good rule is to treat your spouse with the same courtesy you would bestow on a friend, client and boss. It is the little things that count—opening the door for each other, greeting one another enthusiastically when you return from being apart, smiling, waiting until the other person is finished before you speak, asking for help courteously and always saying please and thank you.

Sarah complains, "George is busy on the computer when I come home. I think the house could fall down around him and he wouldn't notice. The kids can be screaming, and even when I yell for help he won't budge."

George counters, "I get finished as fast as I can. If you would stop yelling at me to do this, then that, I would be finished sooner. I think I do a lot more than most men. I clear the table, wash the dishes, clean the kitchen, help the kids with homework, take my turn doing their baths and help put them to bed."

Sarah retorts, "You do the job, but you don't listen to what is going on. There is more to the evening than routine jobs. You are out of it. You only think of yourself."

George looks up to the ceiling and rolls his eyes and with an exasperated sigh says, "See, it's never enough."

Initially, George refused to see his behavior as disrespectful. When asked what he did when his boss or a client walked into his office while he was working, he grimaced and admitted he would stop working, stand up, walk toward them, smile and reach out his hand. He admitted that if he treated them the way he treated Sarah, he would be fired.

And would Sarah yell insults at one of her coworkers if they weren't doing what she expected? Hardly.

Should your lifetime partner, the person you love and with whom you created a family, be treated with less respect than a boss or client?

My advice to George and Sarah was to make it a point to be polite to each other and to work toward these goals:

- Stop, look, listen and learn when your partner is talking to you. Stop what you are doing, look at them and listen. Surely you have time to look and listen for a few seconds to the one you love.

- When you are not able to communicate, go toward your partner, touch them lightly, look them in the eye and politely ask for help.

- When you are having a recurrent problem, schedule prime time to work out a plan to resolve the issue.

- Think about the way you treat your partner, and ask yourself if you treat others better. If you do, start holding yourself to a higher standard, daily!

Generally we know what good manners are, even when we don't choose to behave well. The gestures my clients report appreciating the most:

- A warm smile
- A loving greeting. Stopping what you are doing, standing up, walking toward your spouse, smiling, hugging and saying hello or good-bye
- Eye contact (especially while talking)
- Saying, and meaning, please and thank you

Common sense says you cannot have a successful working relationship if you are rude. Neither can you have a healthy, productive marriage without good manners. Be courteous in the way you talk to each other. Watch the tone of your voice. Is it warm, loving and caring or cold, rude or hostile?

It takes a little effort and forethought, but these little kindnesses add a great deal to creating an affair-proof marriage.

▼ BE PLAYFUL

Couples who play together, stay together.

Being each other's lover includes laughing, loving—and playing with each other. Having fun together does not require complicated arrangements or expensive toys, but it does take thinking, planning and making play a priority. Put some energy into this. Romantic lifetime loves are not effortless. Go beyond your comfort level. Do something different.

Each couple I surveyed had the word *romance* on their list of the qualities they wanted in their marriage. I love the dictionary definition of romance: idealized love; tender or intimate mood; fanciful; to make more pleasing, inspiring, exalted; highly exciting; raising to a higher level than is purely realistic.

Doesn't that sound great? Well, maybe not all the time, but some of the time. It is important to make a marriage something special. So here are some ideas if you want a marriage that is tender, intimate, fanciful, inspiring, pleasing, exciting, exalted and at a higher level than is purely realistic!

50 Ways to Be a Lover

1. Share a bubble bath and sip champagne.
2. Lightly run your index finger around the edges of her face.
3. Play Frisbee.
4. Buy and play a CD of love songs.
5. Find a song that is "our song" and play it often.
6. Cup her face in your hands, look into her eyes and say, "I love you."

7. Read your lover a short story, or a poem.

8. Make love outdoors.

9. Run your fingers through his hair.

10. Go out to see a romantic movie once a month.

11. Whisper a joke to your lover in public (be a little naughty).

12. Listen to a romantic song, and dance at home!

13. Play strip poker.

14. Spend a day in bed laughing and loving.

15. Leave a note on the dishwashing detergent, "You are my joy," or "Thoughts of you cheer me up."

16. Have a picnic in bed.

17. Light a candle and take turns undressing each other—one article of clothing at a time!

18. Use massage oil or a simple lotion, and give each other a back rub.

19. Get tickets to his favorite game and go along enthusiastically.

20. Feed each other finger foods by candlelight.

21. Flirt and court. Pretend you just met, and seduce each other.

22. Send a romantic cards to him at work.

23. Write a love note every month.

24. Send an invitation through the mail asking for a special date.

25. Select some sexy underwear for each other and wear it out on a date.

26. Use your lipstick to write words of love on his mirror.

27. Look through a lingerie catalog together and let him show you what he likes.

28. Men love lingerie–buy it and wear it!

29. Buy a sex toy and play with it together!

30. Caress his face, shoulders, arms and then hands.

31. Put a note on the car seat saying, "I'll miss you today."

32. Snuggle.

33. Initiate a hug a day, make it last a full minute.

34. Take her favorite drink—wine, martini, coffee or tea—to her hairdresser and have it served while she is having her hair done. (PS: tip the hairdresser $20).

35. Leave a loving message on her voice mail.

36. Fill a basin with warm water, soak her feet in it, gently lift one foot at a time and gently dry it with a towel, and then caress her foot while you massage in her favorite lotion.

37. Collect and watch romantic videos. Here are some of my clients' favorites: *The Bridges of Madison County, Ghost, Casablanca, French Kiss, Sleepless in Seattle, Somewhere in Time* and *Out of Africa*.

38. Play catch.

39. Massage his hand slowly and sensually with unscented lotion.

40. Wash her hair.

41. Give her flowers every month (remember the song "You Don't Bring Me Flowers Anymore").

42. Dance together. If you don't know how, take lessons together.

43. Surprise her with a little present, beautifully wrapped.

44. Whisper your favorite line from your love song in her ear.

45. Cuddle.

46. On a lamp, put a note that says, "You light up my life."

47. Kiss in the park.

48. Go for a horse-drawn carriage ride.

49. Make love somewhere other than the bedroom.

50. Reserve a room in a local hotel. Give her a single red rose along with a written invitation to a romantic rendezvous. Make all the arrangements.

Romance is risky and a little silly—that's why it's exciting. The little things we do that are out of our normal routine are memorable. Excitement comes from going beyond normal boundaries. Try it and have fun with each other.

Doris wondered, "Maybe what I want is unrealistic. I want us to be the way we used to be. Not all the time, just now and then."

Jack answered, "Come on. After ten years the fire dies; that's just the way it is. We have a good marriage. Quit worrying."

Doris didn't quit worrying, because she felt some stirrings deep within her for Joe, a management consultant who was temporarily working in her office. Doris got scared when she found herself looking forward to Joe's calls and dressing up on days when she would see him. She did not want to have an affair. Her sister had had an affair, and Doris did not want to go through the pain she saw her sister experience.

Somewhat reluctantly, Jack agreed to work on making their marriage more special. Here is what they did:

▶ Scheduled a date night once a week, which they took turns planning. The only rule was that it had to be something they had not done before.

▶ Set a midweek rendezvous for sex or making love. They

agreed at least to try something new. Doris brought out an old book, *The Joy of Sex*, for ideas.

► Shared a daily laugh. Joe loved jokes, so he listened for jokes to tell Doris and he bought a joke book to draw from.

► Flirted. Flirting had been fun for Doris when they were dating, so she decided to flirt with Joe over dinner by looking into his eyes (he used to say he felt like she was looking into his soul), smiling and whispering compliments to him even when they were the only two in the room.

► Adopted a code to signal each other when they wanted some intimate time (not necessarily sexual). T-time. Time to talk and touch tenderly.

Within a few weeks Doris and Jack had a romantic marriage. Jack admits he was skeptical that he could rekindle the passion he had felt for Doris years before, but he has. "Actually, I feel more in love with her and more turned on to her then ever before," he says. "She's on my mind all the time. It's great."

Being each other's lover means laughing, playing and loving together. Lovers are easily fascinated and delighted by the joys of the moment. Put the struggles and hassles of your daily life aside and feel the joy of each other's presence. It doesn't take long—fifteen minutes, maybe half an hour. Touch and talk tenderly—it's T-time! Look deep into the eyes of your lover. Talk about what you see; it's OK to be mushy!

If you want a playful and fun marriage, work at it. If you want a romantic marriage that is tender, intimate, fanciful, inspiring, pleasing, exciting, exalted and at a higher level than is purely realistic, it takes thought, skill, imagination, dedication, daring, planning and scheduling.

▼ PLAN

Creating a happy, healthy, affair-proof marriage takes planning, and planning takes time, energy, thought and scheduling. If you want an intimate, romantic, lifetime marriage, get out your schedule, or create a calendar, and block out time for each other. Think about the qualities that you want your marriage to have, identify the behaviors that lead to those qualities and write them on your calendar. Schedule something every day— big or small doesn't matter, but some gesture of love every day. We schedule time for everything else that is important in our lives. Time for each other is no less important than a business meeting or the ballet.

Making love is important in maintaining an affair-proof marriage. When we are twentysomething we have plenty of those hormones running around in our brains to drive us easily and frequently to a state of frenzied passion, but realistically after a few years of marriage it just doesn't happen like that—at least not often enough! Schedule time for love. Once I convince my clients to try it, they don't go back to relying on spontaneity for talking, touching, playing, being romantic or making love.

▼ SUMMARY

Remember the five Ps for affair-proofing your marriage— be protective, positive, polite, playful and have a plan. Protect your marriage by staying out of situations that are risky. Be positive and catch your partner doing something right. Be polite; good manners are a sign of respect. Be playful; couples who play together stay together. Make plans for love-making and romance and schedule enough time.

Affair-proof your marriage and have fun. Once a week

create a date night. Take turns planning it. Make it fun, something a little out of the ordinary. Instead of going out to a restaurant, go on a picnic. Go out of your way to do something romantic for your partner. Choose from the list of 50 ways to be a lover, or make your own list and schedule the time. Decide what you will do daily and weekly to make your marriage loving, affirming, adventurous, supportive or romantic.

Beyond the serious aspects of a marriage, there should be time, energy and enthusiasm for fun, pleasure—and play. Make time to be each other's lover.

Conclusion

Generously love one another—each and every day!

Affairs—love affairs and sex affairs—have been part of life since antiquity and they will be part of the future. There is a biological basis for the drive to mate and to mate again. Every culture throughout recorded history has attempted to find a social formula to accommodate the desire of human beings for multiple mates without creating social anarchy. In recent years, divorce has been the acceptable way of selecting new mates.

When I started my research on affairs, I did not expect the evidence to be so lopsided. I have seen the intensity of love, passion, desire and intimacy affairees have for each other. I know it is real. I know that the intentions of most affairees are sincere, but the data and my counseling experience say that the long-term prospects for happiness are not good.

Over and over I see women wait through their childbearing years for their lovers to leave their wives. As the timeworn adage says, "Men don't leave their wives and marry their lovers." After a few years, either the affair becomes as stable as a long-term loving relationship, or it ends in pain and disappointment.

Occasionally an affairee will leave a marriage and marry a

lover, but the prospects of a happy, long-term marriage are very, very low; around 80% to 90% fail. It is a hard way to start a life together. The feelings driving the relationship will lessen, and the complexity of life increases. While there are many guesses as to why so many affair-marriages fail, the bottom line is that very few succeed.

Affairs rarely have happy endings. Someone or everyone gets hurt. After the first edition of this book was printed, Suzy came to talk to me about a discovery that had shattered her faith in people and her confidence in herself. She admitted she had always thought her husband had a lover, but she had refused to confront her suspicions.

Suzy and Jay had moved into their neighborhood shortly after the birth of their first child. Eric and Helen, their next-door neighbors, were also new to the city and had a baby the same age. Suzy and Helen helped one another with the joys and trials of parenting, always being there for one another. When Eric and Helen had two more children, they decided to remodel their house rather than move away from Suzy and Jay. They were a great foursome. They had their children at the same time, vacationed together and shared their innermost secrets. They were best friends, their children more like brothers and sisters than neighbors.

At forty-five, Jay had a massive stroke and died immediately. Suzy didn't know if she would have survived without Helen and Eric. As always, Suzy turned to Helen and Eric for strength, comfort and love.

A few months after Jay's death, a box containing his personal files arrived from his office. Early one evening while the kids were doing their homework, Suzy started sorting through the box. As she flipped through the papers, she recognized Helen's handwriting on the outside of an envelope. She opened it and started reading the card inside. She felt a cold chill run through her as she read Helen's love letter to Jay. She found love letter after love letter in the plain brown box. She read on, through descriptions of rendezvous, lovemaking, anecdotes about her and Eric, words of love and passion. Here was the intimacy she had longed for, but never found with Jay. Suzy tore through the box looking at notes, letters, cards and photographs spanning twenty years.

Suzy grabbed a handful of letters and pictures and stormed over to confront Helen. Helen cried and tried to explain that she and Jay did indeed love each other, but had agreed that everyone was better off if they remained with their own families. Helen tried to explain that both she and Jay also loved Suzy—it wasn't a lie. Suzy simply could not listen to Helen. She went home and told her children, showing them the letters. She called Helen and Eric's kids and again revealed the letters.

Astonishingly, the response from her kids was that "Helen and Jay always did seem more like they were married while you and Dad were friends." Suzy was shattered. She could trust no one.

Helen and Eric remain married, but they are struggling. Their children and Suzy's children continue to try to figure out how to be friends. Their entire support system is in shambles.

When I spoke to Suzy, she admitted to ignoring many problems. When she was jealous or hurt she hid her feelings. When she thought Jay was seeing his lover, she made snide comments, but she didn't want to force the issue. She didn't want to make Jay mad, because she was afraid he might leave.

Some argue that Suzy was better off to ignore her suspicions of the affair and keep her marriage together. That was certainly an option. She could have decided to accepted the affair and keep her family intact. When she discovered the letters, she could have destroyed them. The problem is, Suzy didn't make a choice. She refused to confront the problem, because she was afraid of being alone. As is often true, fears became reality. Suzy built her whole world around her fear of being alone. When Jay was gone, her entire world was gone with him. Now Suzy, Helen, Eric and their children are confused, angry, betrayed and alone.

I'm telling you this sad story to remind you to face your fears—experience a painful revelation or admit a devastating truth. Have your crisis in the present; don't postpone it for your future. Pay attention to problems, and address your concerns, worries or fears. It is common for affairs to occur with people we know—a colleague, a coworker or a friend. If you have a problem or a suspicion, resolve it. Don't let it linger.

A marriage can only be as good as your communication and is safe only when it is tended to daily. Couples who actively listen, make it a point to understand what their partner is saying and respond with acceptance and caring even when they disagree have the strongest marriages. That does not mean they are emotionally flat. Couples have different styles: some confrontive or volatile, others affirming and subtle. It doesn't matter what your style is, as long as you can listen and care about what each other thinks and feels, and are able to solve problems and create solutions that work for both of you.

Women are drawn to affairs to meet self-esteem needs: wanting attention to the inner self, wishing to be understood emotionally and desired physically. Men typically seek affairs for sex initially, but over the long term they want to be enjoyed, appreciated and respected. Women usually meet their self-esteem needs verbally, while men often meet those same needs physically. Know and meet your spouse's needs—willingly and enthusiastically.

Overall, men and women want the same things from their marriage—best friends, love, romance, sex and support. There is a difference in how men and women get their needs met. Women want love and understanding, so tune in. Snuggle with her and listen to her thoughts, her feelings and her concerns. Use simple, brief phrases that show you are listening and that you care. For instance, try using these simple phrases: "Yes, it is really a difficult problem," or "Gosh, I don't know what I would have done," or "It sounds like you handled it well." Remember, no advice!

Men want respect and appreciation for being a provider and for their contributions to your quality of life. They often want it expressed physically. Sex, yes, but also touching and casual affection. Touch a man and watch his reaction. Now, lightly touch his neck or his cheek, look into his eyes and tell him you appreciate how he takes care of you. You'll get his undivided attention in a heartbeat.

Like it or not, it is essential to be protective of your marriage. Marriage is probably the most important investment we make, but we have a tendency to be careless rather than careful. Stay out of situations that lend themselves to intimate contacts. Trust your intuition. If you feel you or your spouse is in danger, don't dismiss the feeling. You are probably right. One study reported that when wives believed their husbands were having an affair, they were right 75% of the time.

Pay attention to your partner. Stop, look, listen and learn. When marriages begin, we are filled with hope and optimism. We see each thing our partner does and says in a warm and glowing light. Qualities of which we aren't especially fond we think of as charming idiosyncrasies or signs of character. It is important to work to keep this attitude later in marriage, to search for the good in each other, and to be generous with approval, acceptance and praise.

Lovers make each other a top priority. They are careful to spend quality time together. They are considerate of each other and interested in each other's feelings, thoughts and ideas. They express joy, delight and love during the time they spend together. They plan and schedule time for sex, time for talking and time for play. They insulate their relationship from the trivial hassles of life. They make each other feel important. Be each other's lover and you will not have to worry about someone else taking over. Listen to what is important, especially if it seems inane to you. Treat these discoveries as little treasures. They are intimate secrets, and cherishing them says you know how to love your mate.

Add pleasure to each other's life. It is the little gestures and good deeds that create romantic bonds. Bring magic to your marriage by granting each other's wishes. Take care of your marriage, and remember intimacy is built day by day.

Bibliography

Allman, William. 1993. "The Mating Game." *U.S. News & World Report.* July 19:57–63.

Athanasiou, R., Sharver, P., and Travis, C. 1970. "Sex: A Report to Psychology Today Readers." *Psychology Today.* July:39–52.

Atwater, Lynn. 1979. "Getting Involved: Women's Transition to Extramarital Sex." *Alternative Lifestyles.* February 1:33–68.

———. 1982. *The Extramarital Connection: Sex, Intimacy and Identity.* New York: Irvington.

Bell, Robert, and Peltz, Dorthyann. 1973. "Extramarital Sex Among Women." *Medical Aspects of Human Sexuality.* March 3:10–40.

Bellis, Mark, and Baker, Robin. 1990. "Do Females Promote Sperm Competition? Data for Humans." *Animal Behavior* 40(5), November:997–99.

Blumstein, Philip, and Schwartz, Pepper. 1983. *American Couples.* New York: William Morrow.

Botwin, Carol. 1988. *Men Who Can't Be Faithful.* New York: Time-Warner.

————1994. *Tempted Women.* New York: William Morrow.

Bridges, William. 1980. *Transitions, Making Sense of Life's Changes.* New York: Addison-Wesley.

Brody, Jane. 1987. *Jane Brody's Nutrition Book.* New York: W.W. Norton.

Buss, David. 1994. *The Evolution of Desire.* New York: Basic Books.

Campbell, Joseph. 1988. *The Power of Myth.* New York: Doubleday.

Clark, Ronald, and Hatfield, Elaine. 1989. "Gender differences in receptivity to sexual offers." *Journal of Psychology and Human Sexuality* 2:39–55.

Cuber, John. 1969. "Adultery; Stereotype versus Reality." In G. Neubeck, ed. *Extramarital Relations.* Englewood Cliffs, N.J.: Prentice Hall.

Cuber, John, and Harroff, Peggy. 1966. *Sex and the Significant Americans.* Baltimore: Penguin Books.

Ellis, Albert. 1960. *The Art and Science of Love.* New York: Lyle Stuart.

Ellis, Albert (with Robert Harper). 1961. *Creative Marriage.* New York: Lyle Stuart.

Ellis, Bruce, and Symons, Donald. 1990. "Sex Differences in Sexual Fantasy: An Evolutionary Psychological Approach." *Journal of Sex Research* 27(4), November:527–55.

Ellis, Havelock. 1940. *Studies in the Psychology of Sex.* New York: Random House.

Everly, George, Jr., and Sobelman, Steven. 1987. *Assessment of the Human Stress Response.* New York: AMS Press.

Fisher, Helen. 1982. *The Sexual Contract: The Evolution of Human Behavior.* New York: Quill.

————. 1992. *Anatomy of Love.* New York: W.W. Norton.

Fisher, Roger, and Brown, Scott. 1988. *Getting Together: Building Relationships As We Negotiate.* New York: Penguin Books.

Fisher, Roger, and Ury, William. 1983. *Getting to Yes: Negotiating Agreement Without Giving In.* New York: Penguin Books.

Ford, Clellan, and Beach, Frank. 1951. *Patterns of Sexual Behavior.* New York: Harper & Brothers.

Frayser, Suzanne. 1985. *Varieties of Sexual Experience: An Anthropological Perspective on Human Sexuality.* New Haven, Conn.: HRAF Press.

Freedman, Jonathan. 1978. *Happy People.* New York: Ballantine Books.

Gass, Gertrude, and Nichols, William. 1988. "Gaslighting: A Marital Syndrome." *Contemporary Family Therapy* 10(1), Spring:3–16.

Gebhard, Paul. 1980. "Sexuality in the Post-Kinsey Era." In W. Armytage, R. Chester, and J. Peel, eds. *Changing Patterns in Sexual Relations.* New York: Academic Press, pp. 45–57.

Glass, S.P., and Wright, T.L. 1985. "Sex Differences in Type of Extramarital Involvement and Marital Dissatisfaction." *Sex Roles* 12(9/10):1101–19.

———. 1992. "Justifications for Extramarital Relationships; the Association between Attitudes, Behavior and Gender." *Journal of Sex Research* 29(3), August:361–87.

Gottman, John. 1994. *Why Marriages Succeed or Fail.* New York: Simon & Schuster.

Gray, John. 1992. *Men Are from Mars, Women Are from Venus.* New York: HarperCollins.

Gray, Paul. 1993. "What is Love?" *Time.* February 15:47–49.

Hafner, R.J., and Spence, Neil. 1988. "Marriage Duration, Marital Adjustment and Psychological Symptoms: A Cross-Sectional Study." *Journal of Clinical Psychology* 44(3):304–16.

Hall, Trish. 1987. "Infidelity and Women: Shifting Patterns." *New York Times.* June 1:B8.

Halper, Jan. 1988. *Quiet Desperation: The Truth about Successful Men.* New York: Warner Books.

Hatfield, Elaine, and Rapson, Richard. 1993. *Love, Sex, and Intimacy.* New York: HarperCollins College Publishers.

Henriques, Fernando. 1963. *Prostitution and Society.* New York: Citadel Press.

Heyn, Dalma. 1993. *The Erotic Silence of the American Wife.* New York: Signet Books.

Hite, Shere. 1976. *The Hite Report—A Nationwide Survey of Female Sexuality.* New York: Macmillan.

———. 1981. *The Hite Report on Male Sexuality.* New York: Macmillan.

———. 1987. *Women and Love.* New York: Alfred A. Knopf.

Holden, C. 1991. "Depression, the News Isn't Depressing." *Science.* December 6:1450–52.

Hopson, Janet. 1988. "A Pleasurable Chemistry." *Psychology Today.* July/August:29–33.

Hunt, Morton. 1969. *The Affair: A Portrait of Extra-marital Love in Contemporary America.* New York: World Publishing.

———. 1974. *Sexual Behavior in the 1970s.* New York: Playboy Press.

Jankowiak, William, and Fisher, Edward. 1992. "A Cross-Cultural Perspective on Romantic Love. *Ethnology* 31:149–55.

Janus, Samuel, and Janus, Cynthia. 1993. *The Janus Report.* New York: John Wiley & Sons.

Jenks, Richard. 1985. "A Comparative Study of Swingers and Non-swingers: Attitudes and Beliefs." *Lifestyles* 8(1):5–20.

———. 1985. "Swinging: A Test of Two Theories and a Proposed New Model." *Archives of Sexual Behavior* 14(6), December:517–27.

Kelly, E. Lowell, and Conley, James. 1987. "Personality and Compatibility: A Prospective Analysis of Marital Stability and Marital Satisfaction." *Journal of Personality and Social Psychology* 52(1):27–40.

Kinder, Melvyn, and Cowan, Connell. 1990. *Husbands and Wives.* New York: Signet Books.

Kinsey, Alfred C., Pomeroy, Wardell, Martin, Clyde, and Gebhard, Paul. 1953. *Sexual Behavior in the Human Female.* Philadelphia: W.B. Saunders.

Kirsta, Alix. 1993. *The Book of Stress Survival.* New York: Simon & Schuster.

Kriedman, Ellen. 1989. *Light His Fire.* New York: Dell.

———. 1991. *Light Her Fire.* New York: Dell.

Kübler-Ross, Elisabeth. 1969. *On Death and Dying.* New York: Macmillan.

LaCroix, Paul. 1926. *History of Prostitution.* New York: Covici & Friede.

Lampe, Phillip, ed. 1987. *Adultery in the United States: Close Encounters of the Sixth (or Seventh) Kind.* Buffalo, N.Y.: Prometheus Books.

Landi, Ann, 1991. "Who's Happy Now?" *Self.* August:89–91.

Lauer, Robert, Lauer, Jeanette, and Kerr, Sarah. 1990. "The Long-Term Marriage: Perception of Stability and Satisfaction." *International Journal of Aging and Human Behavior* 31(3):189–95.

Laumann, Edward, Gagnon, John, Michael, Robert, Michaels, Stuart. 1994. The Social Organization of Sexuality: Sexual Practices in the United States. Chicago: The University of Chicago Press.

Lawson, Annette. 1988. *Adultery: An Analysis of Love and Betrayal.* New York: Basic Books.

Le Doux, Joseph. 1994. "Emotion, Memory and the Brain." *Scientific American*. June:48–57.

Lewinsohn, Richard. 1956. *A History of Sexual Customs*. New York: Bell Publishing.

Lewis, Hunter. 1990. *A Question of Values*. New York: Harper & Row.

Liebowitz, Michael. 1983. *The Chemistry of Love*. Boston: Little, Brown.

Linquist, Luann. 1989. *Secret Lovers*. Lexington, Mass.: D.C. Heath Co.

Macklin, Eleanor. 1980. "Non-traditional Family Forms: A Decade of Research." *Journal of Marriage and Family*. November:905–22.

———. 1983. "Effect of Changing Sex Roles on the Intimate Relationships of Men and Women." *Marriage and Family Review*, pp. 97–113.

Maslow, Abraham. 1968. *Toward a Psychology of Being*. New York: Van Nostrand.

Mead, Margaret. 1949. *Coming of Age in Samoa*. New York: Mentor Books.

———. 1967. *Male and Female: A Study of the Sexes in a Changing World*. New York: William Morrow.

Meyering, Ralph. 1987. "Decision-Making in Extramarital Relationships." *Lifestyles* 8(2):115–29.

Micholas, Alex. 1994. "On the Road to Happiness." *Psychology Today* 27(4) July/August:32–37.

Moore, Thomas. 1994. "Soul Mates." *Psychology Today*. March/April:27–31.

Neubeck, Gerhard, ed. 1966. *Extramarital Relations*. Englewood Cliffs, N.J.: Prentice Hall.

New Woman. 1986. "Infidelity Survey." October and November.

Newman, J. 1992. "Prevalence of Aids Related to Risk Factors and Condom Use in the United States." *Science*. November 13:5085–96.

Novello, Surgeon General Antonia. 1993. *The Surgeon General's Report to the American Public on HIV Infection and AIDS*. U.S. Public Health Publication.

O'Brien, Pamela. 1993. "The Love Life of an American Wife." *Ladies Home Journal*. February:128–32.

O'Neill, Nena, and O'Neill, George. 1972. *Open Marriage: A New Lifestyle for Couples*. New York: M. Evans.

Ornish, Dean. 1990. *Program for Reversing Heart Disease*. New York: Random House.

Penney, Alexandra. 1989. *Why Men Stray and Why Men Stay.* New York: Bantam Books.

Pesmen, Curtis. 1992. *What She Wants: A Man's Guide to Women.* New York: Ballantine Books.

Pittman, Frank, M.D. 1989. *Private Lies: Infidelity and the Betrayal of Intimacy.* New York: W.W. Norton.

Reinisch, June. 1991. *The Kinsey Institute New Report on Sex.* New York: St. Martin's Press.

Richardson, Laurel. 1985. *The New Other Woman.* New York: The Free Press.

———. 1986. "Another World." *Psychology Today.* February:23–27.

Ripps, Susan. 1993. *A Passion for More.* New York: St. Martin's Press.

Rokeach, Milton. 1973. *The Nature of Human Values.* New York: The Free Press.

Scarf, Maggie. 1987. *Intimate Partners: Patterns in Love and Marriage.* New York: Random House.

Schwartz, Pepper. 1994. *Love between Equals.* New York: The Free Press.

Seyle, Hans. 1956. *The Stress of Life.* New York: McGraw-Hill.

Singh, Devendra. 1993. "Adaptive Significance of Waist to Hip Ratio and Female Physical Attractiveness." *Journal of Personality and Social Psychology* 65:293–307.

Smith, Lynn G., and Smith, James, eds. 1974. *Beyond Monogamy.* Baltimore: Johns Hopkins Press.

Spanier, Graham, and Margolis, Randie. 1983. "Marital Separation and Extramarital Behavior." *Journal of Sex Research* 19(1), February:23–48.

Stark, Elizabeth. 1986. "Friends Through It All." *Psychology Today.* May 20:54–60

Tannen, Deborah. 1990. *You Just Don't Understand.* New York: Morrow.

Taylor, Christina. 1986. "Extramarital Sex: Good for the Goose? Good for the Gander?" *Women and Therapy* 5(2/3):289–95.

Thoits, Peggy. 1983. "Dimensions of Life Events that Influence Psychological Distress: An Evaluation and Synthesis of the Literature." In Kaplan, Howard, ed. *Psychosocial Stress: Trends in Theory and Research.* New York: Academic Press.

Thompson, Anthony. 1982. "Extramarital Relations: Gaining Greater

Awareness." *The Personnel and Guidance Journal* 61(1):102–4.

———. 1984. "Emotional and Sexual Components of Extramarital Relations." *Journal of Marriage and Family.* February:35–42.

———. 1993. "Extramarital Sex: A Review of the Research Literature." *Journal of Sex Research* 19(1), February:1–22.

Toufexis, Anastasia. 1993. "The Right Chemistry." *Time.* February 15:49–51.

Travis, Carol, and Sadd, Susan. 1977. *The Redbook Report on Female Sexuality.* New York: Delacorte Press.

Vaughn, Peggy. 1989. *The Monogamy Myth.* New York: Newmarket Press.

Viddler, G. Clayton. 1993. *The Principles of Seduction: How to Get Another Person to Fall in Love with You.* New York: Pedestal Press.

Viscott, David, M.D. 1977. *The Language of Feelings.* New York: Pocket Books.

Vital Statistics Divorce: United States. U.S. Department of Health and Human Services. Public Health Service and Centers for Disease Control, National Center for Health Statistics. Division of Vital Statistics. 1986.

Wagner, Nathaniel, ed. 1974. *Perspectives on Human Sexuality.* New York: Behavioral Publications.

Wallerstein, Judith, and Blakeslee, Sandra. 1989. *Second Chances.* New York: Tickner & Fields.

———1995. *The Good Marriage: How and Why Love Lasts.* New York: Houghton Mifflin.

Whitehurst, Robert. 1983. "Sexual Behavior in and out of Marriage," *Human Sexuality and the Family.* Ontario, Canada: The Haworth Press.

Wilson, Barbara. 1989. *Remarriage and Subsequent Divorce: United States.* U.S. Department of Health and Human Services. Public Health Service and Centers for Disease Control, National Center for Health Statistics. Division of Vital Statistics.

Wolfe, Linda. 1975. *Playing Around: Women and Extramarital Sex.* New York: William Morrow.

Wright, Robert. 1994. "Our Cheating Hearts." *Time.* August 15:45–52.

▼ RECOMMENDED READING

A Question of Values, Lewis Hunter
Anatomy of Love, Helen Fisher
The Book of Stress Survival, Alix Kirsta
The Evolution of Desire, David Buss
Flow: The Psychology of Optimal Experience, Csikszentmihalyi Mihaly
Getting to Yes: Negotiating Agreement Without Giving In, Roger Fisher and William Ury
Getting Together: Building Relationships As We Negotiate, Roger Fisher and Scott Brown
The Good Marriage: How and Why Love Lasts, Judith Wallerstein
Intimate Partners, Maggie Scarf
Jane Brody's Nutrition Book, Jane Brody
The Language of Feelings, David Viscott
Light Her Fire, Ellen Kriedman
Light His Fire, Ellen Kriedman
Love between Equals, Pepper Schwartz
Men Are from Mars, Women Are from Venus, John Gray
Men Who Can't Be Faithful, Carol Botwin
On Death and Dying, Elisabeth Kübler-Ross
The Power of Myth, Joseph Campbell—video series also available (800–223–6834)
The Principles of Seduction: How to Get Another Person to Fall in Love with You, G. Clayton Viddler
Private Lies: Infidelity and the Betrayal of Intimacy, Frank Pittman
Program for Reversing Heart Disease, Dean Ornish (excellent health resource with a misleading title)
The Road Less Traveled, M. Scott Peck
Second Chances, Judith Wallerstein
Why Marriages Succeed or Fail, John Gottman
You Just Don't Understand, Deborah Tannen

Yuen Lui

LANA STAHELI, PH.D., has been a certified counselor for more than two decades and has helped more than 1,000 individuals and 500 couples. She lives in Seattle, Washington.